I can understand the factors Susan Chapman mentions about "being ready to allow ourselves to be interrupted by God" and circumstances. The factors enumerated by the author prepare us to face such interruptions. I fully recommend the adoption and practice of these very essential requirements for right and appropriate approach to mission work.

Rene' S. Sison
MD. Kabankalan City, Negros Occidental, Philippines

This short book is packed with profound insights that will help us live contended lives in an unideal world. It is biblically based and theologically alert, while helpfully using insights from the behavioural sciences. It is also eminently practical. As I read, I felt I was sitting at the feet and learning from a wise and seasoned servant of God.

Ajith Fernando
Author, *Discipling in a Multicultural World*

This material can be a great help to Christians and Christian workers as they follow the Lord.

Bethel D. Schnitzlein, PhD
Composer, Author, Singer, Lecturer

This small book is a goldmine of pastoral wisdom, forged in personal experience, personal suffering and perplexities, and of course the outworking of many years of honest searching of the Scriptures. Susan Chapman writes with clarity and great honesty, unafraid to expose some of the things over which she has struggled, times of failure, and the often difficult path to humble self-knowledge. She tackles head on some of the specific challenges for those in professional Christian ministry, be they pastors or missionaries. And she provides a thoughtful, biblical route map for navigating those, with concrete steps to deal healthily with the unexpected 'interruptions' that can so easily knock us off balance. Any serious disciple of Jesus Christ would benefit from prayerfully reading this book, or using it for group study.

> Rose Dowsett
> Missiologist and Author

Whose life hasn't been interrupted in the 2020s? Yet we are still thrown off-balance by the unexpected. From her personal wisdom, meditation on Scripture, and knowledge of the human person, Susan Chapman shows us how we can face uncertainty not with stoical resignation, but with faith, hope, and love. This short book is packed with insights from experience, theology, psychology, and more. Chapman reminds us that our limitations are something we must learn to accept as part of being human — but this is not a counsel of despair.

> Michael Jensen
> Rector, St Mark's Anglican Church, Darling Point;
> Author, *Is Forgiveness Really Free?*

This book should be required reading for every Christian seeking to serve cross-culturally or in church ministry. A testimony of a real life experience as a missionary.

> Rev. Bishop Eric D. Maefonea
> Bishop of South Sea Evangelical Church, Solomon Islands

LIFE INTERRUPTED

A REFLECTIVE JOURNEY

SUSAN CHAPMAN

The cover design is an abstract take on the theme of interruption. The rough splatter of paint across a canvas appears like a mistake or a mess for those wanting controlled paint strokes that show clearly what is being represented.

Furthermore, the stark white looks like a negative space with jagged edges jutting out, just like what an unplanned interruption in the painting process might look like.

Yet, there is beauty in such a rough piece of art, if only we look at it from a different perspective. And what we see is but a fragment of the entire painting that God is working on. Interruptions can contribute to what God is doing in our well-planned lives, if we trust that, 'He has made everything beautiful in its time." (Ecc. 3.11)

– Karen Quek, Cover Designer

To those who have shared this journey of life with me as fellow pilgrims, especially Mark. Your practical care and love, particularly over the last year, has (literally!) been a lifesaver. Our shared journey is definitely not dull and boring!

Life Interrupted: A Reflective Journey
Copyright © 2022 Susan Chapman

 aussie.life.interrupted@gmail.com

All rights reserved. No part of this publication may be reproduced, stored in a retrieval system, or transmitted, in any form or by any means, electronic, mechanical, photocopying, recording or otherwise, without the prior written permission of the author, except in the case of brief quotations embodied in critical articles and reviews.

All Scripture quotations are taken from THE HOLY BIBLE, NEW INTERNATIONAL VERSION®, NIV® Copyright © 1973, 1978, 1984, 2011 by Biblica, Inc.™ Used by permission. All rights reserved worldwide.

Scripture quotations marked TPT are from The Passion Translation®. Copyright © 2017, 2018 by Passion & Fire Ministries, Inc. Used by permission. All rights reserved. ThePassionTranslation.com.

Scripture quotations marked TLB are from The Living Bible. Copyright © 1971 by Tyndale House Publishers.

Cover design: Karen Quek
Layout: Graceworks Private Limited
Typeface: Classico, Felt Tip Roman

ISBN: 978-0-645-44220-5

1 2 3 4 5 6 7 8 • 27 26 25 24 23 22

CONTENTS

Foreword	ix
Acknowledgements	xi
Introduction	1
Step 1: Knowing Truth	7
Step 2: Continuing to Grow	35
Step 3: Embracing Appropriate Self-care	49
Conclusion	63
Appendix	67
Bibliography	76
Endnotes	80

FOREWORD

It may be helpful to have a bit of background to this book. The content was sparked by reading and assignments for academic study in mid-2020. The task for the mini-research project was to read widely, identify some common factors that affect ministers/pastors, and then propose how to respond well to these factors by creating a personal development plan. I looked at material regarding both those who work within their own culture and those who work across cultures, and termed them all 'gospel workers'. The influences on these two groups of people were surprisingly similar — with only one difference.[1] The 'personal development plan' formed at that time is the framework of the material here.

These findings, along with insights from other reading, were first pulled together for a ladies' retreat in September 2020 and refined since then. The refining and reflecting led me to think that these insights are helpful and true regarding all who take their Christian faith seriously — not just for 'gospel workers'. With the encouragement of others, this book is presented out of a desire to make it more widely available. It contains both insights and suggestions for personal reflection and group discussion. I strongly recommend working through the material with at least one other person and sharing the journey together. We always benefit when sharing life lessons with each other.

ACKNOWLEDGEMENT

Any writing project takes a community. Even though my name is listed as the author, there are many who contributed to this book. I readily admit that my short-term memory is not good and may forget to include people here. Please do forgive me if this is the case.

The genesis of this book grew out of formal study. Rev Keith Mitchell was the lecturer who prompted reflection on this topic through practical academic assignments. Who says that formal study has to be stuffy and divorced from the reality of life? The ladies organizing the 2020 OMF Ladies Retreat in Thailand invited me to lead their time together, and they suggested Bonhoeffer's quote as we discussed the possible content. Then the men who took part in a re-run of this retreat in the Philippines confirmed that the material was not only applicable to females. That was where things would have stayed, except Nicole Harvey insisted on the value of making the content more widely available by converting it from a retreat outline to a book.

After the upheaval and interruptions in the first half of 2021, when I was wondering if this project was worth pursuing, Jeanette Morris and Dale Jones gave effusive encouragement that the message was timely and worth publishing. Proofreaders gave advice, input and feedback: Lindy Hope, Robyn Lanham, Mark Chapman, Dr. Jo Lynch, Christine Dillon (and I am sure there were others!). Karen Quek helped fine-tune the title and designed the cover.

And Priscilla at Graceworks Singapore gave guidance and help in the final stages.

And through it all, my family — Mark, Hannah and Ruth — listened to never-ending reflections and ponderings, and allowed me to share their stories as part of my own journey. Thanks to all of you from the bottom of my heart.

INTRODUCTION

On the morning of March 5, 2020, I stepped off the shuttle van from Suvarnabhumi Airport to Don Muang Airport in Bangkok. After an overnight flight and stopover in Singapore, I was not at my best — but I smiled at the sight of Mark waiting for me at the departure terminal. We had been married for nearly 30 years, and our lifestyle meant that at least one of us was often travelling. This time it had been a month since we had seen each other. We were heading to the Philippines for just under a week. The conference we were going to lead there had been cancelled, but we chose to still go, and to be available for however God would like to use us. I was looking forward to the time ahead.

Well, the week turned out to be very eventful — a colleague diagnosed with cancer and returning to his passport country for further tests and treatment, Mark making himself available to step into the vacant leadership role, me falling sick, having a Covid-19 test and missing my flight home to Bangkok. Week two entailed being in isolation for two weeks and ringing the hospital multiple times a day for more than a week to get the (thankfully negative) results of the test, Mark carrying two jobs, and Enhanced Community Quarantine being implemented in Metro Manila with travel totally suspended. We, and everyone around us, were trying to work out how to 'do life' in this vastly changed environment. What followed was eight months of working where we were, living in the various levels of community quarantine as the authorities in the Philippines tried to rein in the havoc from the virus. Like millions of people worldwide, we transferred all our work online. The guesthouse we were staying in became an extended household of 6-10 people. There were many opportunities to journey with them (and others virtually) — being available and working with God in others' lives. All this time we were waiting for the door to open to return to our apartment in Bangkok. Remember, we had planned to be away for only one week. We constantly enquired and applied and prayed. And then, in early November, our work permit and visa for Thailand expired; the door shut.

We were exhausted and disappointed in God. We knew he could work wonders. We had seen it in the past. But he had stood by and let our plans and dreams be shipwrecked. Yes, we could see God's timing in many ways. We knew we were serving him wherever we were. But that didn't mean it was easy. It didn't mean we weren't disappointed. We wanted to be able to go home.

Almost 100 years ago, Dietrich Bonhoeffer wrote that, "We must be ready to allow ourselves to be interrupted by God. God will be constantly crossing our paths and cancelling our plans ..."[2] Bonhoeffer was writing about the 'ministry of helpfulness' within any true Christian community, and the need to be always ready for interruption in order to help others — yet there is a wider truth here, a truth that goes far beyond being ready to put down our own plans in order to help someone else.

We make plans and they are interrupted. This is life. And our human nature is to not respond well to these interruptions. It is good to remember that God is God. He is sovereign. Montgomery Boice reminds us that verses like Proverbs

16:9, "In their hearts humans plan their course, but the Lord establishes their steps, "need to be read within the wider context of Proverbs 21:30, "There is no wisdom, no insight, no plan, that can succeed against the Lord."[3]

Even when he doesn't actively interrupt our plans, he allows them to be disrupted. It is wise and prudent for us to respond graciously, meekly, humbly when things go awry — but it is certainly not easy.

Before we go any further, I would like to address a potential concern this may raise. As Bethel Schnitzlein reasoned, "Who are we to say that God interrupts?! He is God, He can do what pleases Him. You and I are His created beings. ... We will have many difficulties and insurmountable conflicts, problems and challenges. This is part of our earthly existence."[4] This is very true, and in the following pages we will explore the rationale for, and wise response to, suffering and failure. Using the sentiment of God interrupting our plans is simply looking at life from our own, admittedly limited perspective, and acknowledging God's sovereignty.

So, how can we be prepared to respond well — to be ready to allow ourselves to be interrupted? Here are three steps to help us. These are not the all-encompassing 'how to's' that will guarantee success. Nor are they the sure way to always have peace in the middle of the messiness of life. But they are steps that will help us to be prepared.

First, knowing the truth is important. Another way of saying this is to have correct theology — theology regarding ourselves, suffering and failure, and work. The second step is continuing to grow, particularly in emotional and cultural intelligence and cultural humility. The third step is embracing appropriate self-care. This self-care is made up of realistic expectations, self-awareness, wholistic care, a healthy network of relationships, and living wisely within limits.[5]

As I read these steps again, I am thankful that God brought them to my notice last year. They speak truth to my heart regarding my own journey over the past year or so. Being reminded of these at different points has enabled me to navigate our own interruptions well.

Let's look at each step in turn — acknowledging that knowing these steps isn't enough. We need to keep them in mind and put them into action in daily life.

STEP 1
KNOWING TRUTH

Living life well is a lot more than just knowing the truth. Orthodoxy (knowing the truth), orthopraxy (living the truth) and orthopathy (feeling the truth) are all important and work in harmony together. But knowing truth is foundational for living life well. Having correct theology is the important first step in being ready for life to be interrupted.

Each culture and country have different parts of God's truth that are embraced, and parts that are rejected or forgotten. "Every culture has some aspect of Christianity that is very difficult to maintain."[1] I am presenting three facets of truth that have 'rung true' personally, and from my research, are important to affirm, as many of us in the twenty-first century have forgotten them. But it is important to acknowledge that the need for these three particular facets have stood out in a particular historical and cultural context. You may find that the truths outlined below have been ingrained in you through your culture and family values. If this is the case, thank God! But before you skip ahead to step two, take time to ask God to highlight to you which forgotten or rejected truths you need to focus on. Believe me, there will be some. Every culture and family have parts of their narrative and values that need to be brought in line with God's truth.

So, let's dip into the first important element of truth — a theology of self.

A. THEOLOGY OF SELF — WHO ARE WE?

How can we be ready to allow ourselves to be interrupted by God? By being confident in who we are.

We are beloved by God

According to Scripture, we are first of all beloved by God. There are many, many references in the Christian Scripture that talk of God's love for his people. He is a God who has made us in his image. He has chosen to be in relationship with the people he created. He especially has a heart for the outcast, the minorities, those on the fringes of society. I have appreciated Richard Gibson's reflections on this topic, affirming that God's emotions are real and he feels deeply for his people[2]. He points out that our being compassionate and kind mirrors God's love for us. The instruction given to the Ephesians to 'live a life of love' is based on God's example of a "deeply committed and emotional love".[3] Through the research for his PhD thesis, Gibson came to the conclusion that "[t]he whole story of the Bible holds together around these descriptions of the way God relates to people."[4] Pete Scazzero, Parker Palmer, Dallas Willard, Karina Kreminski and many others have also affirmed the need for the protestant, evangelical sections of the church to embrace the spirituality of being utterly beloved by our Creator God.

Gibson came to this conclusion from his study in theology, and others have come to a similar conclusion from psychology and the field of 'mindfulness'. Ben Crowe reminds the athletes he coaches that they are 'human beings and not human doings'. Trent Crotchin points to a career-changing realisation in 2017 that "I'm not perfect ... but I am worthy."[5] Juliet Benner describes it this way — "Christian spirituality is a journey into loving communion and union with God.

It is learning to look into the face of God, and rather than experience guilt, fear or shame, know our belovedness."[6]

In my words, each one of us is worthy because we are human beings, beloved by God.

It is important to note that knowing we are beloved isn't emotional shallowness. Jen Schepens points out from Psalm 139 that it is the basis for being known by God, seen by him, and transformed by him. Because we know we are beloved, we can ask God to search us. Schepens explains that verses 1-6 illustrate how God knows us. Verses 7-16 continue in describing that he sees us, affirming that we are created in his image. And verses 17 and following show how we can come in boldness, trust, humility, and integrity — asking him to search us and let us know what he knows and sees. "Now we can ask for his revelation as we personally examine anything that has gotten in the way of us living out our true identity as his creation."[7]

Embracing and being settled in being beloved leads to healthy self-compassion. When Jesus talked about loving others as we love ourselves, he was repeating a commandment given to the people of Israel hundreds of years earlier.[8] These commandments acknowledge that we do love ourselves, and they stand against the misguided teaching that self-love is wrong. The Bible is clear that self-centredness and egotism are wrong. But self-hate is never the solution to loving others and denying ourselves. The field of psychology has embraced the concept of self-compassion, and there is truth in this. In the words of Kristen Neff, self-compassion is "a way of relating to ourselves kindly, embracing ourselves as we are: flaws and all."[9] Her website explains, "With self-compassion, we give ourselves the same kindness and care we'd give a good friend."[10] To me this sounds like the fruit of knowing, really knowing, and imbibing that I am loved by God. We will pick this thread up again in step two.

Let's look at another aspect of the truth: we are finite.

We are finite

Alongside being secure in being loved by God, we need to be totally content in being finite, created beings. God is infinite. We are not. This truth is not one I imbibed naturally through life. Os Guinness reflects that I am not alone in this: "Modern life assaults us with an infinite range of things we could do, we would love to do, or some people tell us we should do."[11] He then points out God's truth in this regard: "Having made us as human beings, he [God] respects our humanness and treats us with integrity. That is, he treats us true to the truth of who we are. It is human beings and not God who have made spirituality impractical."[12]

In 2013, when asked, 'How is life going?', I remember replying, 'There are so many possibilities and opportunities in life. I wish there were two of me.' Then I came across the writings of Ruth Hayley Barton regarding the importance of being content in our limitations. The phrase was, 'living graciously within God-ordained limitations.' I have been revisiting this concept during 2021. These limitations come in many forms and from many sources — most of which we do not have control over. When our children were small, the limitations were on physical rest and sleep, and being able to choose what I would like to do for a holiday. Over the last year, like many around the world, there have been limitations in travel and whom I can visit, even for major life events. Having a malignant tumour removed has brought limitations of health and energy. This year has continued, for many of us, to be one full of unexpected and unwelcome happenings. My prayer has daily been, 'Lord, enable me to be content within my finiteness and limitations — and to allow you to be the unlimited, sovereign one.'

This extended quote from Ruth Hayley Barton has a lot of 'meat' in it. I encourage you to pause as you read it, and consider how it applies to you:

> Living graciously within the boundaries of our life as it has been entrusted to us gives our life substance. Oddly enough, something of the will of God is contained in the very limits that we often try to sidestep or ignore. Living within limits is not in any way an acquiescence that is despairing, passive or fatalistic. Rather it honours the deepest realities of the life God has given us. Life in this body at this age and stage. Life in my family at its age and stage. Life in this personality. Life with this community. Life in the midst of this calling.[13]

Let me put this in my own words: It is okay to be limited, to be finite. That is how it is meant to be. Since God is the creator of all, only he is infinite and unlimited.

We are 'reciprocating selves'

The third part of knowing who we are is a concept called being 'reciprocal selves'. Balswick, King and Reimer explain that "[h]ow we are conformed to Christ occurs through and results in mutual, reciprocal relations with God, humans and creation."[14] This is based on a theology of the Trinity, that with God the Father, Son and Holy Spirit, we see what Balswick et al. call "particularity and relationality" in reciprocity. The Father, Son and Spirit are different, separate. Yet they are also in harmonious relationship, and who they are is formed by their relationship together.[15] This gives us a pattern for our own selfhood. I am who I am in relationships.

Relationships form me and call responses out of me. I am both alive and formed in relationship with others. As a reciprocating self, I acknowledge that relational contexts are important to who I am, and that I am part of others' relational contexts.[16] In Ajith Fernando's words, "Christianity is a communal religion. Everything that we do is communal".[17] I have described this in theological, Christian terms, but it is not only Christian thought that has come to this conclusion. Brené Brown starts her now famous TED talk on the, 'Power of Vulnerability', with the axiom that "connection is why we are here … neurobiologically it is how we are wired."[18] Johanna Lynch comes to a similar conclusion from her research as a medical physician on whole person health. She states that it is wise to see "humans as multi-layered — incarnational embodied people embedded in environments and communities of interconnected relationships. … We are woven together with love. We know that love through our senses and our connections to others and our world."[19]

Woven together with love: this relationality flies in the face of the rampant individualization in many minority world cultures.[20] It means I embrace that my selfhood, who I am, is intrinsically entwined with those around me.

Alongside relationality is the concept of particularity. The majority of cultures represented by the minority world embrace individualization and in general affirm particularity. Scazzero identifies a potential danger within Christian marriages in leaning too far into relationality, highlighting the need for particularity in what he calls 'differentiation'. He points out the danger of co-dependence, having our responses and behaviours controlled by others and their actions.[21]

Being a reciprocal self entails steering clear of the two opposite dangers of complete individuality and co-dependence, and embracing both relationality and particularity. Tweaking Scazzero's description of co-dependence above, being a reciprocal self means that our responses and behaviours are influenced, but not controlled, by others and their actions.

Conclusion

These three aspects unpack some important truths regarding who we are. To conclude, let's turn them into a simple prayer:

Lord, thank you for the truths that we are beloved, finite, and reciprocating selves. Help us to settle into these truths, to feel comfortable in them. Please continue to speak to us in this. Amen.

Reflection

- Here is a guide for an individual and communal reflection time to explore our theology of self.

- By yourself, start with a time of meditation to quieten your spirit. 10–15 minutes is a helpful length of time. If it is helpful, use a resource like the *Daily Lectio Divina* podcast, or the *Examen* app, or a website to guide you through a time of visio divina, such as https://www.prayerandpossibilities.com/pray-with-eyes-of-the-heart-visio-divina/.

- After this time, reflect on the questions below:

    1. How do you struggle with each of these?
    - Being beloved
    - Being a limited, finite created being
    - Being a 'reciprocating self'

    Whatever struggles have come to mind, bring them to God.

    2. How does each of the three above challenge you?
    3. How does each release or affirm you?
    4. List any actions that God is asking you to do or stop.
    5. To conclude, thank God for how he has spoken to you.

- If you are sharing your journey with others, what story about yourself would you like to share in the discussion time? It can be any story about who you are.

- When you meet, choose someone to be in charge — to

keep people on track and to ensure everyone is prayed for. Each tells a story (suggestion is 10-15 minutes) about who you are. Others are to just listen. After the story is finished, have one person pray, thanking God for this person. Repeat until everyone has told a story and been prayed for.

B. WHEN THINGS DON'T GO TO PLAN

Part of knowing truth is having a robust theology of both suffering and failure. This enables us to have healthy foundations and assumptions when life doesn't go to plan.

We can be ready to allow ourselves to be interrupted by God by first being confident in who we are. This is part of a theology of self. Building on this, we can have clarity regarding God's perspective on things going wrong. This is the theology of suffering and failure.

The reality of life

Having life interrupted is uncomfortable. It can be painful. But it is the reality of life. This reality is easier for some cultures to accept than others. If our culture values planning and clarity then accepting that there are things we cannot control can be confronting. If we have come from a privileged economic background where we have been able to have many choices in life, then this reality is very threatening.

But let me say it again. Life in this world means that things we have planned don't happen and things we don't plan do happen. Earlier I gave an outline of our journey during 2020. Since then, life was certainly not straightforward. It continued to be out of our control in many ways. Jumping ahead to November 2021, we had been here in Australia a year, way longer than we had expected — and still not able to get back 'home' to our apartment in Bangkok.

During this time, we have seen time and time again that it is right for us to be here in this country for now. Life and work have continued as we set up house in an apartment under my parents' house in Brisbane. I was able to attend my graduation and receive an academic prize in person. We had the chance to get to know Charlie, boyfriend to Hannah, our eldest daughter — then be part of the thrill of their engagement, and the months leading up to and including their wedding. There have also been difficult times: Hannah's diagnosis of a degenerative arthritic condition; our other daughter Ruth managing numerous health challenges; then while I was staying with Ruth in Sydney, the discovery and removal of a tumour deep in my back. Our plan was to head back to Brisbane to join Hannah & Charlie's engagement party in July, but the state of Queensland shut the borders to those who had been in Greater Sydney because of a Covid-19 outbreak. When we did make it to Brisbane, I faced further surgery and an extended time of recovery from a significant cavity wound. In September, the wedding was full of joy and a wonderful celebration, but Ruth was still studying in Sydney, and not able to join due to travel restrictions. I was also managing pain and limited movement throughout the day. With our return to Thailand delayed due to my health, we opted to move into our own townhouse when the tenant moved out. There is much about the future that we just don't know. Life continues to be interrupted.

We can see from Jesus' life that not everything went the way he expected or planned it to. Part of his humanity is that he didn't control other's choices. When many of his disciples turned back, he turned to the twelve with him and asked if they also wanted to leave him. There are times when he tried unsuccessfully to have time by himself or just with a few people. Some refused to keep his work secret and caused massive upheaval to his plans. Jesus, being fully God as well as fully human, didn't sin. But he did have bad days — days when things went wrong, when perspective was lost, when he questioned, when he was overwhelmingly sad, when he pleaded with his Father for another path to be opened to him. From this I am confident that these things aren't sin.

Let's look at another example from the Bible. In Exodus 15, we read of Moses leading the people of Israel. They have just seen the ten plagues in Egypt, God's deliverance of them from slavery there, and the amazing crossing of the Red Sea in the sight of the army of Egypt. Verse 22 says, *"Moses led Israel onward from the Red Sea into the Wilderness of Shur. For three days they trekked through the wilderness without finding water."*

Three days for the whole community without water. This is not a punishment because of their disobedience. It isn't because they misheard God's voice and went in the wrong direction. Moses, as their leader, didn't get side-tracked. After the Red Sea victory, they went straight into a difficult time. For this, as for many situations in the reality of life, I don't know the why of the situation. For our situation right now, I also don't know what will happen. BUT, I am confident in some truths. These truths are important to imbibe for the times when things fail — when they don't work out, when God interrupts our plans, and also when we ourselves make a mess of things. These truths I call a theology of failure and of suffering.[22]

Theology of Suffering

As followers of Jesus, we imitate him in many ways. One of these is how we imitate Jesus through suffering. Tim Chester talks of suffering as, 'one of the 5 S's', of taking up our cross and following Jesus — sacrifice, submission, self-denial, service, suffering.[23] Our own cultural background greatly affects how we approach suffering, and it is good to examine this. Pursuing suffering is not a biblical teaching, but neither is avoiding or discounting suffering. Ajith Fernando clearly teaches the two marks of a faithful Christian life are both joy and pain.[24] In 2017, he summarized this as something he has focused on over many years. "I've tried hard ... to talk about how joy and suffering can be there together in our life."[25] None of this should catch us by surprise as part of the journey as a disciple of Jesus. Quoting Fernando again, "We haven't learned to understand that frustration is a part of life. ...and if we don't understand that, we are going to be very unhappy people, because life is frustrating."[26] It is helpful to consider our own attitude towards suffering as a follower of Jesus, and what aspects from our own culture we may have accepted without question.

In my own context of Australia, I often hear Christians take the words Paul wrote in Romans 8 when praying for someone going through suffering. This passage has wisdom and truth, but it can also be used incorrectly and unwisely. "And we know that in all things God works for the good of those who love him, who have been called according to his purpose."[27] One incorrect use is to take this to mean 'in God all things are good for us', when in fact the intention is more 'God can work anything, no matter how bad, to have some good for us in it'.

Following Jesus means imitating his attitude towards suffering. He didn't pursue it with a 'martyr's mindset'. When he knew that he was about to experience heavy suffering, he even struggled to accept it — but Jesus did accept the suffering. He didn't run away from it. One of the writers of the New Testament urges us to look to Jesus, "the pioneer and perfecter of faith. For the joy set before him he endured the cross, scorning its shame, and sat down at the right hand of the throne of God."[28]

Dietrich Bonhoeffer talked of the importance of carrying the cross that is given to us as part of the cost of discipleship. "Jesus says that every Christian has his own cross waiting for him, a cross destined and appointed by God. Each must endure his allotted share of suffering and rejection. But each has a different share ..."[29] Following Jesus may involve all kinds of suffering and death: to popularity, to pride, to racial or national prejudice, and to comfort. What is clear is that, as someone who is committed to trusting and obeying God, suffering will be part of our lives. It is important for us to consider what it means to prepare ourselves to 'walk in the way of the cross'.

Reflection

- Focus on something of beauty that brings you joy. Sit with this joy for a while, and thank God for it. Ask him to give you clarity and wisdom as you reflect.

- Read the passages of Scripture listed below. Read them slowly, a few times each, asking yourself how your own personality and culture affect your approach to suffering.
  - Philippians 1:29-30
  - Colossians 1:24
  - Matthew 16:24-25
  - Hebrews 12:2

- Read them again, asking God to highlight what he wants you to embrace and apply personally.

- Looking ahead to the next six months, what could be a way of the cross for you? Commit this journey to God, asking for his grace.

- Finish this time by listening to 'You're Still God' by Philippa Hanna.
  https://m.youtube.com/watch?v=kUOxKdfQ3zs

- If you are sharing your journey with others, choose something from your personal meditation you would like to share. I.e., How does your personality and culture impact how you approach suffering? What did God highlight to you from the passages of Scripture?

- Pray Hebrews 12:2 for each other, using what you have learned about each other in the prayers.

Theology of Failure

Let's now look at a theology of failure. There are four things that are important to grasp: first, that not all failures are sinful.[30] This diagram outlines five truths regarding life that all contribute to the fact that not all failures are sin. These will be easier or more difficult for us to accept depending on our personality and culture. Some may seem totally logical and common-sense to you. Rest assured that they are not so logical to everyone. I encourage you to reflect on each one of these truths, wrestling with them if needed.

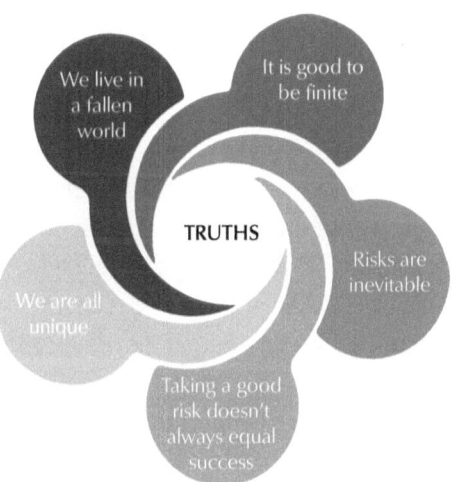

It is good to be finite. "God takes delight in his image bearers, in all their created humanness — including their finiteness."[31] We are limited in our knowledge, in our physical location (one place at any one time), and in our power. This finiteness means that there are some things we will fail at doing.

Risks are inevitable. It is very interesting to look into the history of the concept and meaning of risk. It is linked to moving away from a paradigm of fatalism and predetermined outcomes. If you are more interested in the topic, enjoy where a simple internet search may take you. For now, let's affirm that because God gave us free will and didn't create us as automatons, and because there are both evil and good spiritual realities, then any decision we or others make entails risk.

Taking a good risk doesn't always equal success. Part of living well in this world entails being aware of the risks, taking them into account, and 'taking a good risk'. This can be a choice to ask someone to marry you. Or to ride a difficult track on your mountain bike that you have been training for. The possibilities are endless. Of course, some risks we take aren't wise. As we reflect on the outcome, we learn more and more about ourselves and taking good risks. But since we are finite, and many things are outside our control, even when we have taken a good risk, it doesn't guarantee success in what we are aiming to achieve. We may still fail.

We are all unique. Each person on this earth is made in the image of God. Each one is beloved. Yet we are all different. Each one is unique. Some things that others have the natural ability to do, I will never be able to learn. And some skills come naturally to me and not others.

We live in a fallen world. Ever since mankind turned our backs on God in the beginning, the whole of creation has paid the price. Things are not as they should be; not as they were created to be. Natural and man-made disasters happen. Calamities are often a combination of both. We face consequences of our own sin and wrong decisions, and that of others.

Here is a personal example of these truths in action: In September 2014, after living in the Philippines for most of the previous twenty years, my family and I had been back in Australia for three months. I had driven across town to a Bible College for an interview as a prospective mature-aged student. This is the city I had lived in as a teenager and young adult. I got lost on the way and so arrived late. I drove up the winding driveway on the side of the hill and found the parking spaces at the top were full. I couldn't turn the car around in the space available, so I had to back the car down the driveway.

Despite having been a driver for about 25 years, we had only owned this vehicle for a few months and I wasn't confident in the car's size or turning circle. It took FOREVER to reverse back down the driveway, and then park the car on the street below. When all this was done, I sat in the car and cried, hitting the steering wheel with my hands in frustration. I was such an idiot! Such a failure! How could I have gotten lost? Why didn't I give myself extra time? I had driven for years in horrendous traffic conditions in Metro Manila. How could I be such a bad driver?

In this situation, there were definitely things that I could have done better. And believe me, I made changes in my behaviour as a result — including always having a map to follow when driving. But the point of this story is to describe an event where I failed, where things didn't go to plan, yet it wasn't sin. And therefore, the fitting response is not to feel guilty and run to God for forgiveness, but rather to reflect and learn from the mistakes. Not all failures are sinful. As one of my favourite characters in the series 'The Hawk and the Dove' was described, "[he] could see the difference between human weakness and human sin."[32]

The second thing to note in a theology of failure is that failure that is wilful sin is dangerous. Not all failure is sin. But some is. Anything that goes against God's Word and will is sin. There is no sense in playing down sin and calling it 'just a mistake'. Yet there is a difference between sin and wilful sin. Let's explain this a bit more.

One of the wonderful things about Filipino languages is the ability to be specific in the grammatical forms by adding a few letters to the verb. Did I do the action, or cause it to be done? Am I focusing on me, or on the action, the item used, or whom I am giving it to? My absolute favourite in these specific forms of grammar is: is the action intentional or accidental? In one of the languages, when this is applied to the word 'sin', you get these two words: *nakasala* and *nagpakasala*.[33] *Nakasala* is when I sin, yet there is no premeditated desire or plan. You could say it is 'falling into sin'. *Nagpakasala* is intentional sin and it is extremely dangerous. Look at these two passages from the Bible and the warnings they give.

> Sin is a dethroned monarch; so, you must no longer give it an opportunity to rule over your life, controlling

how you live and compelling you to obey its desires and cravings. So then, refuse to answer its call to surrender your body as a tool for wickedness. Instead, passionately answer God's call to keep yielding your body to him as one who has now experienced resurrection life![34]

No one who lives in him keeps on sinning. No one who continues to sin has either seen him or known him. Dear children, do not let anyone lead you astray. The one who does what is right is righteous, just as he is righteous. The one who does what is sinful is of the devil, because the devil has been sinning from the beginning. The reason the Son of God appeared was to destroy the devil's work. No one who is born of God will continue to sin, because God's seed remains in them; they cannot go on sinning, because they have been born of God.[35]

Note the words used: continuing to sin, yielding and surrendering your body, and keeping on sinning. This intentional turning our backs on God, this *nagpakasala*, is incredibly dangerous. It eats away at our conscience and erodes the motivation to come to God for his restoration. Never underestimate this danger.

The third part of a theology of failure is to embrace that all sinful failures can be forgiven by God. Whether sin is intentional or unintentional, forgiveness is offered. None is too small and insignificant, and none is too large and horrendous. This is part of the radical aspect of God's nature — he is willing to forgive ALL sinful failure. He forgives by grace. It is a gift from him, not earned or won in any way. Through his forgiveness, we are justified. Since we are justified, we can have peace.

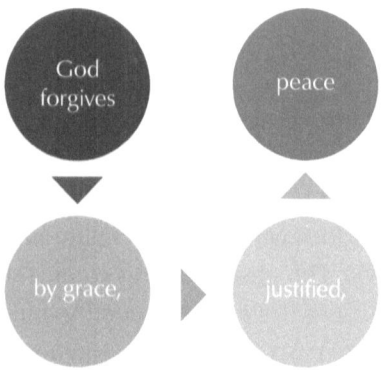

As a child I remembered the explanation that justified is being seen 'just-as-if-I'd' never sinned. I realize that there is debate regarding this explanation and acknowledge that it oversimplifies this meaningful concept. It misses some of the depth of our being credited with Jesus' righteousness as well as our sins forgiven; it can gloss over the reality that payment did have to be made for the enormity of our sins and was made by Jesus; and it totally misses the need for Jesus to continue to be our mediator.[36] Let me say this clearly, justification is different to an acquittal or quashing of a conviction. We are guilty. The punishment is taken by someone else. The outcome is that our slate is clean – the punishment is no longer ours to carry. Hence, we can be at peace.

King David of Israel wrote in Psalm 4, "Now, because of you, Lord, I will lie down in peace and sleep comes at once, for no matter what happens, I will live unafraid!"[37] It was while we lived in the Southern Philippines that I realised the treasure and privilege of living under this understanding. We can lie down in peace not because we know what the next day holds, not because we can guarantee that nothing bad will happen, but because of God. This peace is both peace from concern regarding what may happen to me, and peace from my own regrets and disappointments.

One day in the late 1990's I was feeling really down. I can't remember what I had done, but it was something that I had caused. I felt absolutely wretched. We were staying at a guesthouse, and a dear friend, an experienced cross-cultural worker, gave me some fantastic advice — 'Susan, don't beat yourself up over it. Sure, you made a mistake. You stuffed up. You did wrong. Accept it. Face it. Ask forgiveness and let it go. Satan wants you to keep beating yourself over the head with this. Don't cooperate with him.'

The fourth part of a theology of failure is that God's grace covers it all. His grace covers all failure. Melissa Weissenberger helpfully highlights that when we have a specific expectation of what God's grace looks like, we can miss it. Paul had to learn this, as told in 2 Corinthians 12:9, "Each time he [the Lord] said, "My grace is all you need. My power works best in weakness.' "(NLT) Paul wanted and was expecting the problem to be removed. God gave grace in a different way — grace through the pain, rather than by relieving it. Weissenberger speaks of "walking through deep loss and finding Christ in that lonesome space, with an embrace abundant in empathy, understanding and solace."

And she concludes that it is good to consider how we are "personally, locally, socially, politically, denominationally, or globally expecting a specific grace with limited and rigid expectations that were not given by the Spirit." God's grace is always there, but it is not always as we expect it to be.[38]

Remember these four things: not all failures are sinful; wilful sin is dangerous; all sinful failures can be forgiven by God; and everything is covered by God's grace. If you are someone who likes things represented in diagrams, this diagram of a theology of failure may be helpful.

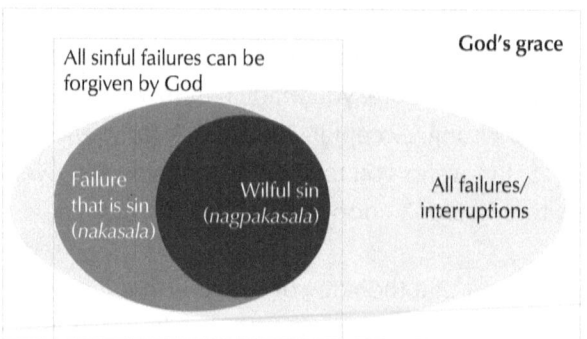

Conclusion

Being interrupted by God is uncomfortable. But it is reality. It is God's way. This is sometimes part of just living in this world. It is sometimes a result of our own sin, or someone else's sin. It is sometimes part of suffering as a follower of Jesus. Scripture is full of stories of failures. It is part of being human. God's grace is always there. What is really important is how we respond.

Reflection

- Find somewhere where you can quieten your heart before God.

- Think of one aspect of who he is, and let that fill your mind. Ask him to guide your thoughts.

- Read Psalm 51 and 1 Kings 19:1–18.

- Read the passages again, asking God to bring things to mind — what is he saying to you about failure?

- Respond to what he is saying.

- Thank God for how he has spoken to you.

- Write, draw or take a photo that you can use as an anchor — to remind you of how God has spoken to you in this time.

- If you are sharing your journey with others, ponder these prompters for your conversation: What stood out to you from today's focus? How can others in this group help you?

- When you meet, ensure someone is in charge to keep you on track.

- Pray Psalm 4:8 over each other.

C. HOW MUCH DOES MY WORK / MINISTRY MATTER?

How can we be ready to allow ourselves to be interrupted by God? Step one is knowing truth. We correct our theology by first being confident in who we are (a theology of self). Then, having clarity regarding God's perspective on when 'things go wrong' (a theology of suffering and of failure). The third part of step 1 — thinking correctly — is considering our perspective on work/ministry (a theology of work/ministry).

This builds on and refers back to the other two parts. Because I am confident in who I am, and because I have clarity regarding God's perspective when things go wrong, I am shielded from overvaluing and undervaluing what I do.

What we do matters to God. He wants us to honour him in all that we do. This means both choosing not to do that which dishonours him and to do any task in a manner and attitude that brings honour to him. No task is too menial or worthless. In God's eyes there is no division of sacred and secular careers. Undervaluing what I do is the danger of saying, "this isn't important to God. It can't be really useful to him." This goes against Biblical teaching and example, and the wisdom of many Christian leaders through the Centuries.[39]

An equal and opposite danger is overvaluing work. This is a particular danger for those whose work is considered 'vocational' and in particular those who are pastors, ministers and cross-cultural Christian workers. What we do is always secondary to who we are. Our identity is in who we are, not what we do. Yet, for those who are ministers, it is a real temptation to overvalue the task of journeying with others in their walk with God. This also conflicts with Biblical teaching and example. Jesus was scathing in his critique of the religious leaders of his day, because they had let their 'ministry' become more important than who they were.

Let's review what we have covered so far — I am beloved, finite, and a reciprocating self. Failure and suffering are part of life for many reasons. These two things blend together in the truths that my work matters and can glorify God; and, no matter how God-glorifying my work or ministry is, it is not my identity.

Reflection

- Read a psalm slowly as a way of preparing for this time. Some suggestions are Psalm 23, 40, 100.

- Consider your perspective on work/ministry.
  - Which of the two dangers are you more likely to fall into — undervaluing it, or overvaluing it?
  - What truths in God's Word help you to keep a godly perspective on your work?
  - How can others help you stay clear of the dangers of undervaluing and overvaluing your work?

- If you are sharing this time with others, give them a summary of your insights from the reflection time.

- Pray over each person in the group. Don't ask them what to pray for, but rather turn a section of Scripture into prayer for them. Here are some possibilities: Joshua 12:7-9. 1 Corinthians 13:4-8, Galatians 1:3-5, Philippians 1:2.

STEP 2
CONTINUING TO GROW

Step one is knowing truth. Building on that, step two is continuing to grow in specific ways. Growth is good and helpful in general, but my research highlighted a particular type of growth that is important if we are to be ready to be interrupted by God.[1]

A. EMOTIONAL INTELLIGENCE

Emotional Intelligence (EQ) can be described as the ability to handle your own emotions and to aptly respond to the emotions of others.[2] The term itself first appeared in the 1960's, and became popular through the 1990's as an aspect of intelligence that had been overlooked in its importance. Here is a quote from the website of the education department of Victoria in Australia.

"Developing emotional intelligence skills helps young people succeed. Study after study has found associations between high levels of EQ and success, for example:

- a major Asian bank found that EQ was a better predictor of workplace success of its employees than IQ
- in a study of USA Air Force recruits, EQ was the best predictor of success
- in a study of 286 organisations where job competencies of star performers at every level were analysed, the most powerful predictors were the EQ skills of awareness, self-regulation, self-motivation, empathy and social skills
- friendship skills also predict successful romantic relationships."[3]

It is this particular area of growth that stood out as being crucial to being able to respond well when life goes 'pear shaped'.[4] A number of Christian writers have concluded that it is impossible to be spiritually mature without being emotionally intelligent.[5] In other words, a lack of EQ will always hamper spiritual growth.

The good news is that we can work on improving our EQ. It can be described as having five competencies: knowing one's emotions, managing emotions, motivating oneself, recognising emotions in others, and handling relationships.[6] The first three competencies deal with handling our own emotions. To grow in EQ, we first look at recognising our own emotions, then we can work on being able to manage them well, then maintaining motivation to appropriately manage our emotions long term. The other side of EQ, responding appropriately to others' emotions, is seen in the fourth and fifth competencies. To grow in these, we learn to recognise the emotions of others; and then, by responding well to them, we work on a healthy handling of relationships.[7]

An interesting topic to explore is Jesus' EQ. Oswald and Jacobson look at the behaviour of Jesus through the lens of EQ. Throughout their book, they work through various areas of EQ in the life of Jesus: self-awareness, empathy, assertiveness, optimism, stress resilience, loving one's enemies, and forgiveness. I don't agree with everything they say, but reflecting on the topic highlights the importance of being aware of and in control of our own emotions.[8]

When considering emotions, it is important to counteract the unhealthy assumption that 'negative emotions' such as anger are ungodly and should be suppressed. Our understanding of the role of emotion is quite different now from the 1980s and 90s. We no longer say that emotions become "damaged". The take away from that outdated teaching was that we were to avoid the "negative emotions" because they were supposedly bad for us. The current healthy advice and practice is to acknowledge both the negative and positive emotions and to respond to them well. Minimising or negating our negative emotional messengers is what can actually lead to many problems.

A number of Christian psychologists and counsellors are concerned that Christians have not been taught well on emotional management. Unhelpful teaching perpetuates the outdated understanding that negative (sad) emotions are bad and to be avoided.[9] A very helpful, current understanding of both positive and negative emotions is explained by Dr Meryem Brown in a podcast from May 2021.[10]

I realize that this exploration of growing in EQ has been very cognitive in its focus, which is quite ironic considering the topic! Please let me stress that EQ is not just a 'managing' of emotion — as that can lead to an unhelpful controlling, quashing, or disregarding of emotions. EQ intrinsically includes a creative and sensory element. To have healthy EQ requires a self-awareness, a sensing of one's own state of being — physical sensations as well as feeling emotions.

Dr. Johanna Lynch has helped me to appreciate that EQ requires a feeling of safety so we can grow in this awareness of what we are sensing.[11] In a Christian's worldview, this safety springs from knowing that we are beloved (Recall step one. See how foundational that is?). When we feel safe, we are able to uncover (individually and in community)[12] what our emotion is trying to warn/inform/change inside us. If you are interested in exploring this characteristic of EQ, take a look at Brown's 'Whole Hearted Inventory' and the ten guideposts of wholehearted living.[13]

We have covered a lot under this topic of EQ. It is good to take time to reflect before we move on to the related concept of Cultural Intelligence (CQ).

Reflection

- Sit quietly and clear your mind of distractions.

- Recall one of the names of God, and focus on this aspect of his character.

- Ask him to guide your time of reflection.

- Take time to describe your 'state of being' right now — your emotions, mental state, and your physical sensations. What do you learn from how you feel?

- Review the five competencies of EQ. Where can you see some growth that God has brought in these areas? Thank him for that.

- Which of these areas of growth is God prompting you about?

- If you are sharing your journey with others, decide what you would like to share. How can they help you in your growth in EQ?

- Pray for each person in response to what is shared.

B. CULTURAL INTELLIGENCE

For those of us who are living and working outside our passport countries, it is obvious that EQ by itself isn't enough. For gospel workers who are working in diverse cultural situations, the reality of managing these EQ competencies, "lived out in multiple contexts where they are communicated in very different ways, leads to a multiplied complexity — a reality of multiple layers of emotional intelligence."[14] In this way, EQ morphs into the more nuanced and complicated Cultural Intelligence (CQ).[15]

My opinion is that CQ is important for everyone in today's world. Let me say this again, with emphasis. I believe that every single person who is living for God's glory in today's world needs to take CQ seriously. The time is long gone when people could say, 'I am living within my own cultural context, I don't need to consider CQ'. I say this for two reasons. The first is that there are very few places in the world today where your neighbours, co-workers and friends come from exactly the same cultural background as you. David Livermore realised this over a decade ago. The primary audience for his book *Cultural Intelligence: Improving your CQ to engage our multicultural world*, published in 2009, was not leaders of multinational corporations or cross-cultural workers, but youth workers and pastors in North America. The first section of the book is focussed on reasoning why CQ is important for these readers.

The second reason why CQ is important for everyone is the reality of disempowered subcultures within societies. The

Black Lives Matter and #MeToo movements are two recent examples of sectors of society that have been sidelined by others who have been empowered by the cultural norms. I do not want to go into the reasons why some are disempowered and others empowered, nor explore our individual or corporate historic contribution to the current situation. The reality is that today, some within our society have greater access to privilege than others. There are real power dynamics at play in every community. And this means that some are disempowered, voiceless, sidelined, disenfranchised, outcast, and overlooked. Please realise that my heart's desire is not to see a totally egalitarian society. In fact, there can be a lot of benefit in healthy hierarchy. What I would love to see is God's heart for the outcast, which is seen in many places in Scripture, to be lived out day by day by his people.

Back in the mid 1980's, David Augsburger termed this interpathy a condensing of *inter-cultural-empathy*.[16] If you are interested in digging more into this concept, Augsburger's explanations and descriptions are a helpful blend of psychology and theology. He highlights some practical guidelines from what he calls 'Rahner's dictum'. This was published by Karl Rahner in 1983 but is timelessly helpful in today's world. It starts: "There is no love of God that is not, in itself, already a love for the neighbor; and love for God only comes to its own identity through its fulfillment in a love for neighbor."[17] Hmmm ... this sounds very similar to some biblical authors:

- James — If you claim to be religious but don't control your tongue, you are fooling yourself, and your religion is worthless.[18]

- John — If anyone claims, "I am living in the light," but hates a fellow believer, that person is still living in darkness.[19]
- Micah — ... what does the Lord require of you? To act justly and to love mercy and to walk humbly with your God.[20]

You see, as a part of God's global family anywhere in the world, I have a responsibility to look out for those who are overlooked by others, and to advocate for them. To do this requires CQ, as I need to apply EQ from a perspective that is different from my own. Whether it is called interpathy, CQ, or any of the other terms used, "It gives you the skills needed to work and relate effectively with people from different backgrounds in your own backyard."[21]

There are a number of models of CQ. Livermore's four-part description of CQ provides a helpful framework for personal assessment and growth.[22]

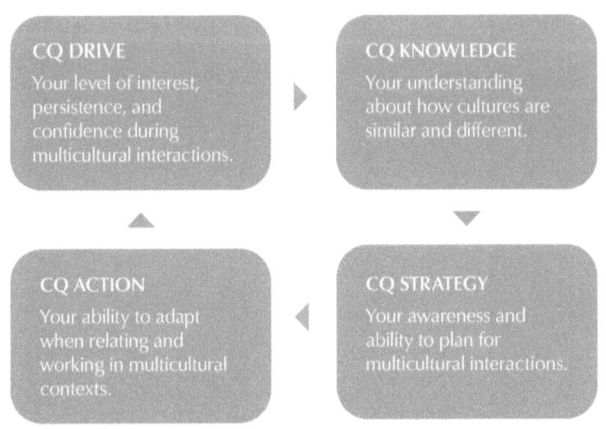

CQ knowledge is a common starting point — finding out about others. Next is CQ strategy, applying that knowledge to be aware and plan for interactions with others. CQ strategy leads to CQ action, putting it into practice in the context where you are as you relate with others. This then leads to CQ drive, providing long-term motivation so we persist in trying and growing in our CQ.[23]

Note that Livermore's model has the arrows between the four components of CQ continuing to cycle, showing that CQ requires ongoing learning. This is extremely important as it mitigates against the danger of CQ. This danger is why I add another layer on to EQ and CQ, and prefer to talk of the need for Cultural Humility.

Reflection

- Sit quietly and clear your mind of distractions.
- Recall one of the names of God, and focus on this aspect of his character.
- Ask him to guide your time of reflection.
- Consider your own living context and environment — who are the disempowered? How can you start to grow in CQ in your relating with them?
- Review the four capabilities of CQ. Where can you see some growth that God has brought in these areas? Thank him for that.
- Which of these areas of growth is God prompting you about?
- If you are sharing your journey with others, decide what you would like to share. How can they help you in your growth in CQ?
- Pray for each person in response to what is shared.

C. CULTURAL HUMILITY

The danger of CQ is that preparing well and focusing on the competence of CQ can lead to losing a humble, learning mindset. It is to say, in effect, 'I am culturally intelligent, I have learned how Asians / women / Europeans / indigenous people / (insert description of the minority here) are similar or different to me. I have planned for interaction well.' And then to forget that this is an ongoing cycle of always learning. We need to continually learn for a number of reasons — because we make mistakes, because cultures are constantly changing and evolving, and also because each person is an individual with their own journey.

Cultural Humility (CH) is a concept that originates from the field of physical healthcare and focuses on the need for self-humility for this paradigm of ongoing learning.[24] It reminds us that interacting with those different to ourselves entails "a lifelong commitment to self-reflection and self-critique."[25] The important distinction is to cultivate an ongoing, lifelong process of self-awareness and reflection, rather than simply discovering and responding to cultural norms and behaviours.[26]

Louise Giesbrecht describes CH as having three dimensions: a mind set, a heart set, and a skill set. Below is a summary of her definition as outlined in a video produced in 2013.[27]

The Mind Set (knowing)

- Self-awareness — healthy knowledge/understanding and awareness of one's motives, attitudes and emotions
- Cultural awareness

The Heart Set (being)

- Self-esteem
- Self-monitoring to carefully consider situations and others when speaking or acting
- Empathy — feeling for others
- Open-mindedness — not having just one set way of thinking
- Reserved judgment — not to easily make judgments about others without careful thinking

The Skill Set — intercultural agility skill (doing)

- Message skills — know how to communicate clearly (verbal or written) to different people/cultures
- Appropriate self-disclosure — to be honest in conversation but also sensitive
- Behavioral flexibility — to be able to adjust your behaviour depending on other/situations/cultures
- Interaction management — know how to keep a conversation going

Reflection

- Sit quietly and clear your mind of distractions.

- Read Philippians 2:3 and 4 meditatively, asking for a humble and teachable spirit.

- Ask God to guide your time of reflection.

- Read Philippians 2:5-11 or another description of Jesus. Consider how Jesus lived out humility, and how God wants you to grow.

- Review the three dimensions of CH. Where can you see some growth that God has brought in these areas? Thank him for that.

- Which of these areas of growth is God prompting you about?

- If you are sharing your journey with others, decide what you would like to share. How can they help you in your growth in CH?

- Pray for each person in response to what is shared.

STEP 3

EMBRACING APPROPRIATE SELF-CARE

We now come to step 3 — embracing appropriate self-care. This can only come after knowing truth and continuing to grow, as it is shaped by them and rests on them. It is important to note that personal care is a strong indicator of long-term sustainability for Christian ministers across various countries — whether working in their own cultural context or cross-culturally.[1] I haven't researched the correlation of self-care to spiritual health of Christians in general, but my assertion is that it is important for all of us, and is a third step for us to be ready for whatever life throws at us.

What is being described here is appropriate self-care. It is not self-idolisation and also avoids the opposite hazard of self-penance and self-hate. The five aspects outlined below all came out of a wide range of reading from various sources.

'OPEN HANDS' APPROACH TO LIFE

Appropriate self-care starts with an 'open hands' approach to life. This term I learned from Meryem Brown.[2] An 'open hands' approach is one that holds plans and even dreams and goals loosely. It is the opposite of a 'closed hands' approach to life that tries to hang on to control of what will happen. There are many stresses as a part of life, especially in a world that is now described as VUCA — volatile, uncertain, complex, and ambiguous. The Covid-19 pandemic has highlighted this to many people who had previously felt that life was fairly predictable. But even before Covid, life has been uncertain and out-of-control for millions of people around the world. It is only those of us from economically and politically stable situations, with the blessing of good health, who were under the impression that we were in control.

Let's take some time to explore what is not meant by this way of living life. An 'open hands' approach is not defeatist. It is acknowledging the reality that there are times when all you have control over is your attitude. Viktor Emil Frankl, a Viennese psychiatrist who survived the Holocaust, spoke from personal experience and professional training when he concluded, "everything can be taken from a man but one thing: the last of the human freedoms — to choose one's attitude in any given set of circumstances, to choose one's own way."[3] If you are interested in seeing what this looks like in action, I strongly recommend Edith Eger's powerful combination of personal memoir, others' stories, and psychological textbook.[4] This isn't just for major trauma survivors. Ash Barty, the Australian world number one tennis player, describes this as a key to her ability to stay focussed when things are going wrong in a match: "I decide my mindset. I decide my attitude. I decide my self worth."[5]

This 'open hands' approach to life is also not aimless. We have already seen how Jesus showed extreme flexibility in many ways, and responded to the situations and people around him. He lived an 'open hands' life. Yet Don Allsman reminds us that "when people tried to get Jesus to turn his attention to their provincial concerns, he stayed focused on the Father's cosmic purposes and re-directed their attention to what is important ... having a single-minded focus on the

Father's work, a tender concern for the marginalized, a habit of forgiveness and love, and a deep satisfaction in God regardless of the circumstances."[6] I believe it is possible to live life as Jesus modelled it — have an open-handed approach to life within a clear aim and objective in life.

SELF-AWARENESS

Appropriate self-care is also made up of self-awareness. This links back to EQ, CQ, and CH — which all entail a type of awareness as the first stage. The more we are aware of ourselves, the more we can care for ourselves well. But self-awareness doesn't come naturally. The Johari window is a tool created by Joseph Luft and Harrington Ingham in 1955. After 65 years it is still a valuable resource, giving a visual representation of what you and others know (and don't know) about yourself.

JOHARI WINDOW

	Open Self	Blind Self
	Hidden Self	Unknown Self

My knowledge →
Others' knowledge ↓

There are multiple YouTube and Vimeo short explanations available. It is worth while taking the time to explore this in regards to your own situation.

Along with the Johari Window, it is important to realise that there are two types of self-awareness — internal and external. Internal self-awareness is a recognition of ourselves — our personal values, cultural values, physical limitations, signs of physical stress, abilities, emotions, reactions, etc. External self-awareness is being aware of how others view us and our values, emotions, reactions, etc.[7] Both types of self-awareness are important.

Tasha Eurich, writing for Harvard Business Review, summarises the benefit of self-awareness from an objective perspective — "Research suggests that when we see ourselves clearly, we are more confident and more creative. We make sounder decisions, build stronger relationships, and communicate more effectively. We're less likely to lie, cheat, and steal. We are better workers who get more promotions. And we're more-effective leaders with more-satisfied employees and more-profitable companies."[8] Self-awareness sounds like a good idea!

HOLISTIC CARE

This self-care is holistic in nature. It acknowledges and addresses physical, emotional, spiritual, intellectual, and relational needs. A practical example of this is asking questions such as, 'How does this action affect my health holistically?' rather than, 'How does this action affect my spiritual health?'

As people of faith, we need to guard against the tendency to spiritualise life unhelpfully into sacred and secular. Our theology of self and theology of work remind us that all aspects of us are beloved by God, and every work can be spiritual. Similarly, appropriate self-care is holistic care for ourselves.

Steve Biddulph describes us humans as a house with four storeys. The ground floor is everyday life as it happens. The second storey is our emotions and emotional response. The third storey is our logical reasoning and cognitive processing. And there is a fourth storey, a rooftop garden where you can see the sky and the other buildings around you. This level is our spirituality, a connection to things bigger than ourselves. Steve asserts that being holistically healthy is being able to move up and down between the levels as appropriate, not getting stuck on any one storey. He concludes, "You can only function when all four storeys have got their lights turned on."[9]

Research shows that a holistic view of care guards against both burnout and neglect of those who are close to us.[10] Holistic care has the benefit of being helpful both in preventing and being prepared for traumatic events, and also responding well to them.[11]

A HEALTHY NETWORK OF RELATIONSHIPS

Fourthly, this self-care has a healthy network of relationships. A helpful way of describing this is using the model of a 'pyramid of care'. This means recognising the variety of relationships that we take part in, and proactively working towards having a healthy mix of relationships around us.[12] This model illustrates having God at the apex of the pyramid, and myself as an individual in the centre of the base. There are four types of human relationships listed in the four corners of the base.

These relationship types are with family and friends, a spiritual community, lay (non-professional) help, and professional help. Each type of relationship is important. Some are used more often than others, but we need to know how to access each type when it is most beneficial. Reflecting on your own pyramid of care is an extremely helpful exercise when moving into a new context. Having all five in place — the four human relationship types and relationship with God — and in a healthy condition will help ensure we are well-cared for.

LIVING WISELY WITHIN LIMITS

Having these four aspects of self-care then enables us to live within limits — the fifth aspect of appropriate self-care.

Note that we cannot jump straight to this aspect. It builds on the others. Living within limits requires an acceptance of our limitedness as created beings — pointing back to knowing the truth as step one; and it builds on our open-hands approach to life and self-awareness — I know that my response to the situation is what I am in control of, and I am self-aware of my strengths and weaknesses. For the past year, my prayer has often been a cry as I hold firmly to Jesus, 'Lord, enable me to be content within my finiteness and limitations — and to allow you to be the unlimited, sovereign one.' It is only when I am content in my finiteness that I am able to live wisely within limits. Living wisely within limits includes the ability to say no appropriately, to articulate priorities, and to "embrace wise limits".[13]

To say no appropriately, we need to stand against any cultural expectation that our busyness is linked to our significance. Author Brené Brown sums it up well — "If we want to live a wholehearted life, we have to become intentional about cultivating sleep and play, and about letting go of exhaustion as a status symbol and productivity as self-worth."[14] Saying no appropriately also means that we do consider any request carefully, especially when it comes from those we respect and those who care for us. An abrupt 'no' with no consideration or listening to God is not an appropriate no.

Articulating priorities can help us know where to focus our limited capacity. Saying yes to something invariably means saying no to something else. Knowing your own priorities before God gives confidence in these decisions. As we do this, we can, with conviction, embrace wise limits.

Living wisely within limits also entails "that we will build into our lives patterns that demonstrate our reliance upon God."[15] These patterns can also be called godly rhythms, or spiritual disciplines. As I write this, I realise that this is not a radical new insight. These principles and truths have been known for millennia — yet it is still helpful to be reminded of them.

A complication to living wisely within limits is that those who are serious regarding their Christian faith carry a personal disposition to help others. This is particularly true for those who are in any of the 'caring' professions, as it is their job to help others. The combination of these factors in the context of the VUCA world we live in leads to a work and life situation that is predisposed towards burnout. I would like to speak particularly to those who are in the caring professions — this is reality from your work and personal values. It is unwise to try to ignore this. It also seems unwise to try to change reality. My suggestion is an alternative mindset. Rather than expecting to arrange life so you never have any signs of burnout (and feeling that you are failing if you do have signs), change your mindset. Acknowledge that the risk is not in the potential of burnout itself, but it is rather the potential hazards of not seeing the danger signs, and not responding well to them. This means that success is when you a) notice your own danger signs, and b) respond well to them.[16]

In April 2021, as I was telling some new workers in our organisation my personal journey, I mentioned my own experience with depression, and the realisation that I need to ensure that I live life with an emotional margin (by this I mean not being 'on the edge' or at my limit emotionally and with stress levels). As I said the words, a conversation started with myself internally.

A small voice inside my head said, "And Susan, you do not have any emotional margin in your life right now." One of the new workers asked me how I knew if I was close to the edge, living life with no margin.

"Well, the main way my body tells me that it is under stress is that I get mouth ulcers *[to self: and you have had a run of mouth ulcers in the last month]*, and I find I don't have as much patience as normal *[to self: hmmm ... some of Mark's habits around the house have seemed annoying recently]*."

This was not good! So, I rearranged life to make space for a mid-week Sabbath, a day of rest — recognising that weekends were not working in this way. Two weeks later, we received news that Ruth, one of our daughters, was going through a crisis, and we travelled interstate to Sydney to spend time with her. When Mark returned to Brisbane, I stayed to support her.

I noted that the mouth ulcers were back, I wasn't sleeping through the night, and was often not able to keep my concentration to complete a task. So, with the encouragement of my boss, I arranged for extra admin support at work for a few weeks. I took long walks in the sun, had coffee and meandering conversations with friends in Sydney, and asked the prayer triplet I am a part of if we could meet weekly to pray for me.

One day during this time, I asked Ruth to give me a back massage to release a tight point in my back muscle.

"Mum, that's not a tight muscle — it's a hard lump of something else."

And thus began the journey mentioned at the beginning of this book — the discovery and removal of a tumour deep in my back. I still don't know the end of the story. So far, everything seems clear and the focus is on recovering from surgery. Whatever is ahead, I do know that I am in an emotionally healthy place right now because of noting the danger signs in April, and then again in May; and both times making changes.

One final note in regards to living wisely within limits — I believe that it is unwise to expect or even desire a total absence of the signs of movement towards burnout. Instead, a wise response is to use two keys to counteract the two hazards mentioned above. These keys are self-awareness and a healthy supportive network. They have been statistically shown to make a significant difference in regards to burnout.[17] This happens by guarding against exhaustion — emotional, mental, physical, and spiritual — and maximising fulfilment and joy in work and life.

Embracing appropriate self-care entails implementing each of these five elements: an 'open hands' approach to life, self-awareness, holistic care, a healthy network of relationships, and living wisely within limits. It is not easy, but it is worth it.

Reflection

- Start with a time of meditation
  - Sit comfortably. Relax your whole body
  - Call to mind one of the images God uses to describe himself — shepherd, king, father, mother eagle, etc. Consider how God relates to you.
  - Turn these thoughts into prayers of praise.
  - Ask for his Spirit to guide you through the rest of this time.

- Considering appropriate self-care, ask yourself these questions:
  - What barriers are there? What can you do about them?
  - What strengths, gifts and experience has God given you that are helpful in healthy self-care? Write a list. Thank God for each one.
  - Who are your fellow pilgrims, journeying with you in this? How can you be a healthy 'reciprocating-self' with them?

- Thank God for how he has spoken to you.

- If you are sharing your journey with others, prepare to share what your take-away is regarding appropriate self-care. When you meet, ensure someone is in charge to keep you on track.

- To close, pray a blessing over each other — here are some possibilities to use.[18]

- "May you be given more and more of God's kindness, peace, and love." Jude 1:2
- "May God our Father and the Lord Jesus Christ give you his blessings and his peace." Philemon 1:3
- "... May God our Father and Jesus Christ our Lord show you his kindness and mercy and give you great peace of heart and mind." 1 Timothy 1:2
- "... May God our Father shower you with blessings and fill you with his great peace." Colossians 1:2
- "May God bless you all. Yes, I pray that God our Father and the Lord Jesus Christ will give each of you his fullest blessings and his peace in your hearts and your lives." Philippians 1:2
- "May God our Father and the Lord Jesus Christ mightily bless each one of you and give you peace." 2 Corinthians 1:2

CONCLUSION

So, there you have it — three steps to help us to be ready to be interrupted by God. We can't choose the interruptions, nor the timing of them. But we can choose to live life so we are ready for life-interrupted when it does happen. I first formed these three steps as a personal development plan for myself. They have been a lifesaver in many ways over the past couple of years.

These insights are only truly useful if they are put into practice. Reading through them is not enough. Choose what is most helpful to you, ask God for strength, gather supportive relationships around you, and put things into action.
My prayer is that you find this beneficial in your own journey to "pursue him passionately, wherever ... stay[ing] focused for the distance."[1]

Reflection

- In Psalm 46, God says, "Be still and know that I am God." Slow your breathing and match these words with the rhythm of your breathing as you quiet yourself before God.

- Write or record a summary of what has impacted you. Consider what has been most timely for you from the three steps presented here. Choose one thing to act on.

- If you are sharing your journey with others, and I do hope you have been, plan a time of celebration together. When you meet, celebrate the wonderful inheritance that we have in each other as brothers and sisters in God's family. Share something from your personal reflection.

- Pray God's blessing on each other. Here is a suggestion from the Anglican Book of Prayer:[2]

  Lord God,
  > *we rejoice in your greatness and power,*
  > *your gentleness and love,*
  > *your justice and mercy.*
  > *Enable us by your Spirit,*
  > *to honour you in our thoughts*
  > *and serve you in our lives;*
  > *through Jesus Christ our Lord.   Amen.*

APPENDIX

From collating research done by others, I found four factors that affect all gospel workers — those who are pastors/ministers and those who are working cross-culturally:

- Working in an inhospitable context
- Having unhelpful self-expectations
- The reality of a never-ending job
- Fulfilment in the job itself

Even though the research was regarding 'full-time workers' — my gut feeling is that they are probably true for all who take their Christian faith seriously, and live life with their main motivation being to honour God. Note that these factors are the reality. Living with the expectation that we can order life so that they don't impact us is unrealistic and unhelpful. It is most helpful to acknowledge and accept them, and respond well. After considering these four factors, I formed a wise response in three steps. This became the content for this booklet.

Below is an explanation of each factor, and some reflection questions.

WORKING IN AN INHOSPITABLE CONTEXT

First, being in an *inhospitable context*. This factor has a number of facets. By the very nature of the profession, gospel workers are in a position where they face spiritual opposition. The many ways that this opposition demonstrates itself underlines Satan's skill in strategy. He is willing to use any means possible towards his goals. This spiritual warfare is real and has a significant impact on the lives of ministers.[1] Alongside the spiritual opposition, gospel workers often minister within an antagonistic social environment. Even in locations where there has been a heritage of respect for religious leaders, scandals and changing societal values are bringing major change. The age of Christendom, where the church and those who represented the church were central to society and respected, has come to an end.[2] It was noted from worldwide research in 2009 that there was very restricted or no religious freedom in a third of all countries in the world — and the situation has continued to worsen since then.[3]

Working in an inhospitable context

- Spiritual opposition
- Antagonistic social environment
- Within the family of God

Turning to looking internally, within the church itself, there is also often a lack of hospitality towards the gospel workers. Corporate and individual expectations are often unrealistic, self-serving, and counter-productive to the purpose of the church and the role of the minister.[4]

The final facet of the inhospitable context is the weighty responsibility that the gospel worker carries daily. Overseeing people's spiritual welfare, standing in the gap and interceding for those not yet in God's Kingdom, investing in significant life change in others, and doing all in their power to encourage people to change from the Kingdom of darkness to the Kingdom of light — all of these aspects of a gospel worker's job can be exacting and demanding. They add to the inhospitable context.[5]

Unless responded to well, this *inhospitable context* naturally brings an emotional heaviness and weariness. The role of a minister is often self-isolating in regard to relationships. Those who choose to not share deeply with their spouse, or lack healthy networks of care, have the indicators of being unable to sustain long-term ministry in a healthy manner. These indicators are seen physically, spiritually, and emotionally.

UNHELPFUL SELF-EXPECTATIONS

The second factor that emerged was *unhelpful self-expectations*. This is grounded firmly in the question, 'What is success as a gospel worker?' If one's definition of success is results, then comparisons with others are inevitable. Times of meeting together with colleagues become stressful events rather than times of mutual encouragement. What constitutes success relates to the two extremely significant concepts and core issues of identity and shame.[6]

In terms of personality and values, gospel workers often work out of a desire to please. If they are not self-aware, this can easily become co-dependency. It is not uncommon for the gospel worker's expectation of their own workload and results to be more than what others expect of them.[7] A feeling of guilt for their own self-care is very common.[8]

> **Unhelpful self-expectations**
>
> - "What is success?"
> - A desire to please
> - Guilt for self-care
>
> Unhealthiness

If unaddressed, *unhelpful self-expectations* lead to unhealthiness. In North America, the physical unhealthiness among gospel workers from these unhelpful self-expectations was overwhelmingly clear.[9] Interestingly, physical negative effects were not so clear in other contexts. It was clear across all contexts that the effects of unaddressed, unwise self-expectations are disastrous spiritually, physically, emotionally and theologically, leading to a downward spiral of self-expectations, behaviour, and consequences.[10]

A NEVER-ENDING JOB

The reality of a *never-ending job* is the third factor encountered by gospel workers. This is shared by many other 'people-work' professions such as counsellors, social workers, and medical personnel. Employment that is centred on meeting people's needs always entails long hours of work and being on call for urgent situations. The very nature of 'people-work' means that progress in many ways is in the hands of those being cared for rather than those doing the caring. Progress in 'people-work' is also often not easily measurable.

> **A never-ending job**
>
> - The nature of 'people-work'
>   - Progress not easily measured
>   - Success is in the hands of others
> - The actual impact depends on how the first two factors are handled

If a gospel worker has addressed the struggles from the inhospitable context and the unhelpful self-expectations in a healthy way, then the struggles from having a never-ending job are greatly reduced. However, if the responses to the earlier factors encountered by gospel workers are not wise and beneficial, the reality of having a never-ending job leads ultimately to burn-out. Kraft has outlined twelve signs of burnout, starting with a craving to do an excellent job, leading to overwork, and neglect of self, not acknowledging the source of these problems, then amending long-held values and denying problems. Following this is a withdrawal from social engagement, major changes in behaviour, an inability to connect with self or others, and an ever-growing internal emptiness. The final two stages in this progression are depression and burnout.[11]

FULFILMENT

Fulfilment is the final factor impacting all gospel workers. Despite the *inhospitable context*, the *unhelpful self-expectations*, and the *never-ending job*, there is a *sense of fulfilment* in taking part in a meaningful and significant vocation.[12] Gratification and a healthy pride come from walking alongside God and working with him, being part of his work in and among people. Balswick, King and Reimer call this healthy pride 'beta-pride'. They see alpha-pride as arrogant self-inflation, while beta-pride is focussed on behaviours — the pride of doing a job well.[13] Having employment that sees lives changed and has the goal of people living fulfilled lives as God intended — this contributes to healthy beta-pride and adds meaning to the daily tasks of gospel workers. The majority of gospel workers see their work as a vocation, a precious task, given to them by God.

> **Fulfilment**
> - Despite the other three
> - Healthy 'beta-pride'
> - Investing in changed lives
>
> ~~Misplaced focus~~

The main struggle in regard to the factor of *fulfilment* is the undeniable bent to focus on the meaningfulness of the work itself, rather than on the relationship with God that provides such meaning. A healthy relationship with God brings high work engagement and an increase in the resources for ministry. This leads to increased fruitfulness and enjoyment in the work itself. The temptation is for the fruitfulness and fulfilment to become the focus for the gospel worker. As fulfilment in the job blossoms, time being with God is often squeezed out, passion for his presence dwindles and desire wanes for reading God's Word for the minister's own benefit. Emotional satisfaction becomes linked more with ministering to others than living for God as the "audience of one".[14] This is a theological problem at heart, that flows through to spiritual life, emotional stability, and relationships with others. It leads to emotional instability, which in turn affects relationships with others, particularly those close to the gospel worker.

Reflection prompters

- Reflect — how much do each of these factors impact you?

- Listen to or read another gospel worker's life story, and note how these four factors affected them.

- What did God highlight to you from this story?

BIBLIOGRAPHY

Allsman, Don. 'Day 3: Jesus Had a Different Objective'. *Loving Jesus More: 40 Days Devotional Series* (blog), 15 August 2021. https://www.bible.com/en-GB/reading-plans/27331-loving-jesus-more/day/3.

Anglican Church of Australia General Synod. *A Prayer Book for Australia: For Use Together with the Book of Common Prayer (1662) and an Australian Prayer Book (1978)*. Edited by E. J. Dwyer. Mulgrave: Broughton Books, 1996.

Augsburger, David. 'Interpathy Re-Envisioned: Reflecting on Observed Practice of Mutuality by Counselors Who Muddle along Cultural Boundaries or Are Thrown into a Wholly Strange Location'. *Reflective Practice: Formation and Supervision in Ministry* 34 (2014): 11–22.

Balswick, Jack O., Pamela Ebstyne King, and Kevin S. Reimer. *The Reciprocating Self: Human Development in Theological Perspective*. Second Edition. Illinois: IVP Academic, 2016.

Barton, Ruth Haley. *Strengthening the Soul of Your Leadership: Seeking God in the Crucible of Ministry*. Downers Grove: IVP Books, 2008.

Benner, J. *Contemplative Vision: A Guide to Christian Art and Prayer*. InterVarsity Press, 2010.

Bickerton, Grant, Maureen Miner-Bridges, Martin Dowson, and Barbara Griffin. 'Well-Being in Ministry Results Overview'. Sydney: University of Western Sydney, N.D.

Bonhoeffer, D. *The Cost of Discipleship*. United Kingdom: SCM Press, 2015. https://books.google.com.au/books?id=379qCgAAQBAJ.

Brain, Peter. *Going the Distance*. Second edition. How to Stay Fit for a Lifetime of Ministry. Australia: Matthias Media, 2020.

Brown, B. *The Gifts of Imperfection: Let Go of Who You Think You're Supposed to Be and Embrace Who You Are*. Hazelden Publishing, 2010.

Brown, Meryem. 'Navigating Mental Health as a Christian'. Podcast. *Word of Life*. Accessed 18 May 2021. https://wayoflifepodcast.podbean.com/e/episode-6-1621300596/.

Burns, Bob, Tasha D. Chapman, and Donald C. Guthrie. *Resilient Ministry: What Pastors Told Us About Surviving And Thriving*. InterVarsity Press, 2012.

Chapman, Susan. 'Emotional Intelligence'. Moodle. *Reflective Blog*

Assignment (blog), 2 August 2020. https://www.morlingonline.edu.au/mod/forumng/discuss.php?d=1228.

Chester, T. *The Ordinary Hero: Living the Cross and Resurrection in Everyday Life*. Epsom: Good Book Company, 2013.

Cultural Intelligence Center, ed. 'Domestic CQ'. Cultural Intelligence Center, 5 July 2021. https://culturalq.com/about-cultural-intelligence/domestic-cq/.

Eger, Edith. *The Choice: A True Story of Hope*. Ebury Publishing, 2017. https://books.google.com.au/books?id=uBwZDAAAQBAJ.

Eurich, Tasha. 'What Self-Awareness Really Is (and How to Cultivate It)'. *Harvard Business Review*, 2018. http://thebusinessleadership.academy/wp-content/uploads/2019/08/What-Self-Awareness-Really-Is-and-How-to-Cultivate-It.pdf.

Fernando, A. *The Call to Joy and Pain: Embracing Suffering in Your Ministry*. United Kingdom: Inter-Varsity Missions, 2008.

Frankl, Viktor E. *Man's Search For Meaning: The Classic Tribute to Hope from the Holocaust*. Ebury Publishing, 2013. https://books.google.com.au/books?id=EbltAAAAQBAJ.

Gibson, Richard. 'God, Man and Emotion'. Podcast. Word of Life. Accessed 21 April 2021. https://wayoflifepodcast.podbean.com/e/episode-5-interview/.

Giesbrecht, Louise. 'Defining Intercultural Competence'. Web video, 2013. https://www.youtube.com/watch?v=SJqBhLgSNQY.

Guinness, Os. *God in the Dark: The Assurance of Faith Beyond a Shadow of Doubt*. Wheaton: Crossway Books, 1996.

———. *The Call: Finding and Fulfilling God's Purpose For Your Life*. Nashville: Thomas Nelson, 2018.

Hay, Rob, Valerie Lim, Detlef Blöcher, Jaap Ketelaar, and Sarah Hay. *Worth Keeping : Global Perspectives on Best Practice in Missionary Retention*. Globalization of Mission Series. Pasadena, Calif.: William Carey Library, 2007.

Hill, Graham Joseph. *Ajith Fernando: Jesus Driven Ministry*. Video. The Global Church Project, 2017. https://m.youtube.com/watch?v=bT0TmCfGBGQ&feature=youtu.be.

Hoke, Stephen, William David Taylor, and Stephen Hoke. *Global Mission Handbook : A Guide for Crosscultural Service*. Downers Grove, Ill.: IVP Books, 2009.

Holloran, Jennifer. 'Day 24: Rewritten Plans'. *Loving Jesus More: 40 Days Devotional Series* (blog), 5 September 2021. https://www.bible.com/en-GB/reading-plans/27331-loving-jesus-more/day/24.

Imamura, Yuzo. 'The Way of the Cross'. Singapore, 2018.

Kanowski, Sarah. 'Meet Ash Barty's Mindset Coach – Ben Crowe'. Podcast. Conversations. Accessed 1 July 2021. https://www.abc.net.au/radio/programs/conversations/ash-barty-sports-mentor-ben-crowe/13418314.

Kraft, Ulrich. 'Burned Out'. *Scientific American Mind* 17, no. 3 (2006): 28–33.

Lee, Cameron, and Kurt Fredrickson. *That Their Work Will Be a Joy : Understanding and Coping with the Challenges of Pastoral Ministry*. Wipf and Stock Publishers, 2012.

Livermore, David A. *Cultural Intelligence: Improving Your CQ to Engage Our Multicultural World*. Youth, Family, and Culture Series. Grand Rapids, Mich.: Baker Academic, 2009.

Lynch, J.M. *A Whole Person Approach to Wellbeing: Building Sense of Safety*. London: Routledge, 2021.

———. 'Tender Welcome: Sensing Ourselves as Beloved Children'. *Luke's Journal of Christian Medicine and Dentistry* 26, no. 3 (August 2021): 22–24.

Miersma, Patricia. 'Counseling Victims of Human-Induced Trauma'. In *Sorrow and Blood : Christian Mission in Contexts of Suffering, Persecution, and Martyrdom*, edited by William David Taylor, 454–61. Pasadena: William Carey Library, 2012.

Mitchell, Keith. 'Sustainability in Ministry and the Prevention of Dropout for Australian Baptist Pastors Serving in Local Church-Based Ministries'. University of Technology Sydney, 2020.

Neff, Kristin. 'The Space Between Self-Esteem and Self Compassion'. TEDx presentation presented at the TEDx Centennial Park Women, Centennial Park, 7 February 2013. https://www.youtube.com/watch?v=IvtZBUSplr4.

Nikles, Dr. D, and S Nikles. *Cycles of Transformation*. 2nd edition. Australia: Christian Wholeness Framework, 2010.

O'Donnell, Kelly S, ed. *Doing Member Care Well: Perspectives and Practices From Around the World*. Globalization of Mission Series. Pasadena, Calif.: William Carey Library, 2002.

Oswald, Roy M., and Arland Jacobson. *The Emotional Intelligence of Jesus: Relational Smarts for Religious Leaders*. Lanham: Rowman &

Littlefield, 2015.

Proeschold-Bell, Rae Jean, and Jason Byassee. *Faithful and Fractured: Responding to the Clergy Health Crisis*. Grand Rapids: Baker Academic, 2018.

Rahner, Karl. *The Love of Jesus and the Love of Neighbor*. Crossroad Publishing Company, 1983.

Reach Out Australia. 'What Is Burnout?' Reach Out Australia, 2021. https://au.reachout.com/articles/burnout-and-chronic-stress.

Roy, Steven C. *What God Thinks When We Fail: Finding Grace and True Success*. Downers Grove: IVP Books, 2011.

S, J. 'Intercultural Living - Cultural Humility'. Self-Study workbook. Singapore, 2017.

Salovey, Peter, and John D. Mayer. 'Emotional Intelligence'. *Imagination, Cognition and Personality* 9, no. 3 (1990): 185–211.

Scazzero, Peter. *Emotionally Healthy Spirituality: It's Impossible to Be Spiritually Mature, While Remaining Emotionally Immature*. Updated edition. Grand Rapids: Zondervan, 2017.

Schepens, Jen. 'Day 8: Known, Seen, Transformed'. *Loving Jesus More: 40 Days Devotional Series* (blog), 20 August 2021. https://www.bible.com/en-GB/reading-plans/27331-loving-jesus-more/day/8.

Taylor, William David, Antonia Van der Meer, and Reg Reimer. *Sorrow and Blood: Christian Mission in Contexts of Suffering, Persecution, and Martyrdom*. Pasadena: William Carey Library, 2012.

The Power of Vulnerability. Webpage. TEDxHouston. Houston, 2010. https://www.ted.com/talks/brene_brown_the_power_of_vulnerability#t-207682.

Victoria State Government, ed. 'Emotional Intelligence'. Victoria State Government, 7 July 2017. https://www.education.vic.gov.au/about/programs/bullystoppers/Pages/adviceemotionalintelligence.aspx.

Weissenberger, Melissa. 'Day 2: The Unexpected Grace of God'. *Loving Jesus More: 40 Days Devotional Series* (blog), 14 August 2021. https://www.bible.com/en-GB/reading-plans/27331-loving-jesus-more/day/2.

Wilcock, Penelope. *The Hardest Thing to Do*. The Hawk & the Dove 4. Oxford: Lion Fiction, 2015.

Wilkinson, William. 'Reviewing an External EModule', 7 June 2021.

ENDNOTES

Foreword & Introduction

1   The difference was that for cross-cultural workers, the support (or non-support) of their spouse was a significant factor. It was noted in the experience of pastors, but wasn't significant.
2   Dietrich Bonhoeffer, *Life Together: The Classic Exploration of Christian Community*, trans. John W Doberstein (Harper One, 1954), 99.
3   Many thanks to Jennifer Holloran for pointing to Boice. Jennifer Holloran, 'Day 24: Rewritten Plans', *Loving Jesus More: 40 Days Devotional Series* (blog), 5 September 2021, https://www.bible.com/en-GB/reading-plans/27331-loving-jesus-more/day/24.
4   From personal email between the author and Bethel Schnitzlein in December 2021.
5   The content in this booklet comes out of some personal research. See appendix for more information.

Step 1: Knowing Truth

1   Graham Joseph Hill, Ajith Fernando: Jesus Driven Ministry, video, The Global Church Project, 2017, https://m.youtube.com/watch?v=bT0TmCfGBGQ&feature=youtube.
2   Richard Gibson's PHD thesis, *As Dearly Beloved Children* affirms that the Biblical writers and early Christians left a rich account of how God loves us. He explains some of this in the podcast *Word of Life. God, Man and Emotion*. Richard Gibson, 'God, Man and Emotion', podcast, Word of Life, accessed 21 April 2021, https://wayoflifepodcast.podbean.com/e/episode-5-interview/.
3   Ephesians 5:1–2 Follow God's example, therefore, as dearly loved children and live a life of love, just as Christ loved us and gave himself up for us as a fragrant offering and sacrifice to God. Explained more in the podcast. Gibson.
4   Gibson.
5   Crotchin is a famous Australian Rules footballer, captain of his premiership-winning club, Richmond, and winner of numerous awards. For more details see https://www.richmondfc.

com.au/news/583765/30-things-about-trent-cotchin and Sarah Kanowski, 'Meet Ash Barty's Mindset Coach — Ben Crowe', podcast, Conversations, accessed 1 July 2021, https://www.abc.net.au/radio/programs/conversations/ash-barty-sports-mentor-ben-crowe/13418314.

6   J. Benner, *Contemplative Vision: A Guide to Christian Art and Prayer* (InterVarsity Press, 2010), 67.

7   Jen Schepens, 'Day 8: Known, Seen, Transformed', *Loving Jesus More: 40 Days Devotional Series* (blog), 20 August 2021, https://www.bible.com/en-GB/reading-plans/27331-loving-jesus-more/day/8.

8   Jesus was answering a question about which commandment was the most important. He answered with two — "'The most important one,' answered Jesus, 'is this: "Hear, O Israel: the Lord our God, the Lord is one. Love the Lord your God with all your heart and with all your soul and with all your mind and with all your strength." The second is this: "Love your neighbour as yourself." There is no commandment greater than these.'" This is in Mark 12:29-31.

9   Kristin Neff, 'The Space Between Self-Esteem and Self Compassion' (TEDx presentation, TEDx Centennial Park Women, Centennial Park, 7 February 2013), https://www.youtube.com/watch?v=IvtZBUSplr4.

10 https://self-compassion.org

11 Os Guinness, *The Call: Finding and Fulfilling God's Purpose For Your Life* (Nashville: Thomas Nelson, 2018), 228.

12 Os Guinness, *God in the Dark: The Assurance of Faith Beyond a Shadow of Doubt* (Wheaton: Crossway Books, 1996).

13 Ruth Haley Barton, *Strengthening the Soul of Your Leadership: Seeking God in the Crucible of Ministry* (Downers Grove: IVP Books, 2008), 112.

14 Jack O. Balswick, Pamela Ebstyne King, and Kevin S. Reimer, *The Reciprocating Self: Human Development in Theological Perspective, Second Edition*. (Illinois: IVP Academic, 2016), 20.

15 Balswick, King, and Reimer, 20.

16 If you are interested in exploring what entails a healthy relational context, Balswick et al. have a helpful description. "A reciprocating self can develop best in a relational context that is characterized by

unconditional love, commitment, gracing, empowering and intimacy." Balswick, King, and Reimer, 12.

17 Hill, *Ajith Fernando: Jesus Driven Ministry*.

18 The Power of Vulnerability, Webpage, TEDxHouston (Houston, 2010), https://www.ted.com/talks/brene_brown_the_power_of_vulnerability#t-207682.

19 J.M. Lynch, 'Tender Welcome: Sensing Ourselves as Beloved Children', *Luke's Journal of Christian Medicine and Dentistry* 26, no. 3 (August 2021): 22–24.

20 The terms *majority world* (and the corresponding minority world) were first used by Shahidul Alam in the 1990s. The *Minority World* roughly corresponds to the *Global North* as a concept — the countries that have colonised others, forming perceptions and shaping narratives regarding the world; and yet population-wise are in the minority. "The 'Minority World' is home to only ¼ of the world population and controls 4/5th of the income earned anywhere in the world. The 'Majority World', on the other hand, is home to ¾ of the world population, but has access to only 1/5th of world income." https://www.travelfordifference.com/why-third-world-is-outdated-what-you-should-say-instead/

21 Peter Scazzero, *Emotionally Healthy Spirituality: It's Impossible to Be Spiritually Mature, While Remaining Emotionally Immature*, Updated edition. (Grand Rapids: Zondervan, 2017).

22 Some of these insights regarding failure are taken from Roy's writings. Steven C. Roy, *What God Thinks When We Fail: Finding Grace and True Success* (Downers Grove: IVP Books, 2011). The insights regarding suffering are taken from a devotion and e-learning lesson from Yuzo Imamura. Yuzo Imamura, 'The Way of the Cross' (Singapore, 2018).

23 T. Chester, *The Ordinary Hero: Living the Cross and Resurrection in Everyday Life* (Epsom: Good Book Company, 2013).

24 A. Fernando, *The Call to Joy and Pain: Embracing Suffering in Your Ministry* (United Kingdom: Inter-Varsity Missions, 2008).

25 Hill, *Ajith Fernando: Jesus Driven Ministry*.

26 Hill.

27 Romans 8:28 NIV

28 Hebrews 12:2

29 D. Bonhoeffer, *The Cost of Discipleship* (United Kingdom:

SCM Press, 2015), 44, https://books.google.com.au/books?id=379qCgAAQBAJ.

30 Roy, *What God Thinks When We Fail: Finding Grace and True Success*, 82.

31 Roy, 82.

32 Penelope Wilcock, *The Hardest Thing to Do*, The Hawk & the Dove 4 (Oxford: Lion Fiction, 2015), 21.

33 This is in the language Bisaya, or Cebuano.

34 Romans 6:12 (TPT)

35 1 John 3:6-8

36 See these articles for further study. http://www.chrismacleavy.com/2014/07/justification-isnt-just-as-if-id-never-sinned/ , https://ericgeiger.com/2014/10/just-never-sinned/ , https://ruach.wordpress.com/2013/03/26/does-justified-really-mean-just-as-if-i-never-sinned/ , https://www.apuritansmind.com/justification/just-as-if-id-never-sinned-not-really-by-dr-c-matthew-mcmahon/ . I recommend Colin Buchanan's song, *Big Words That End in Shun!*

37 Psalm 4:8 (TPT)

38 Melissa Weissenberger, 'Day 2: The Unexpected Grace of God', *Loving Jesus More: 40 Days Devotional Series* (blog), 14 August 2021, https://www.bible.com/en-GB/reading-plans/27331-loving-jesus-more/day/2.

39 See the teaching of Luther, Calvin, and recent writings such as https://www.theologyofwork.org/resources/what-does-the-bible-say-about-work.

Step 2: Continuing to Grow

1 This research was done regarding those who are 'ministers of the gospel', yet my gut feeling is that the results apply to all who are seriously living for Jesus.

2 There are many resources that unpack this concept. Chapters 7 and 8 of the following book unpack both understanding and developing Emotional Intelligence. Bob Burns, Tasha D. Chapman, and Donald C. Guthrie, *Resilient Ministry: What Pastors Told Us About Surviving And Thriving* (InterVarsity Press, 2012), 101–30.

3 Victoria State Government, ed., 'Emotional Intelligence' (Victoria

State Government, 7 July 2017), https://www.education.vic.gov.au/about/programs/bullystoppers/Pages/adviceemotionalintelligence.aspx.

4 A British expression used to indicate that something has gone horribly wrong with a person's plans, most commonly in the phrase "It's all gone pear shaped." https://www.urbandictionary.com/define.php?term=pear%20shaped

5 Scazzero says, "emotional health and spiritual maturity are inseparable. It is not possible to be spiritually mature while remaining emotionally immature." Scazzero, *Emotionally Healthy Spirituality*, 19. "The emotional competencies of pastors and church leaders are probably the most important factors in pastoral effectiveness." Roy M. Oswald and Arland Jacobson, *The Emotional Intelligence of Jesus: Relational Smarts for Religious Leaders* (Lanham: Rowman & Littlefield, 2015), 2.

6 This is simply one model of EQ. Peter Salovey and John D. Mayer, 'Emotional Intelligence', *Imagination, Cognition and Personality* 9, no. 3 (1990): 185–211.

7 There are many courses, books and workshops that are designed to help you grow in these areas. Often what is most helpful is having a skilled person guide you through these steps.

8 Oswald and Jacobson, *The Emotional Intelligence of Jesus: Relational Smarts for Religious Leaders*, 4. Throughout the book, Oswald and Jacobson helpfully work through various areas of EQ in the life of Jesus: self-awareness, empathy, assertiveness, optimism, stress resilience, loving one's enemies, and forgiveness.

9 This is a summary of a conversation with Dr. William Wilkinson, in June 2021. William Wilkinson, 'Reviewing an External EModule', 7 June 2021.

10 The podcast is in two parts. WOL 6 | Meryem Brown- Navigating Mental Health as a Christian WOL 6 | Q&A with Meryem Brown

11 Lynch outlines a comprehensive view of this sense of safety as a transdisciplinary concept integral to holistic care. J.M. Lynch, *A Whole Person Approach to Wellbeing: Building Sense of Safety* (London: Routledge, 2021).

12 Individually and in community — this is applying the particularity and relationality of being a reciprocal self, from step one.

13 See https://brenebrown.com/wholeheartedinventory/. One of

the guideposts is self-compassion. Remember that concept from knowing that we are beloved in chapter one above?

14 Susan Chapman, 'Emotional Intelligence', Moodle, *Reflective Blog Assignment* (blog), 2 August 2020, https://www.morlingonline.edu.au/mod/forumng/discuss.php?d=1228.

15 Burns et al. follow the two chapters on Emotional Intelligence with two chapters on Cultural Intelligence. Burns, Chapman, and Guthrie, *Resilient Ministry: What Pastors Told Us About Surviving And Thriving*, 131–68. Note that there are many names for similar concepts. In 2017 I counted at least twenty-six terms used since the 1940s to refer to the concept of CQ. These include Cultural Competence, Intercultural Sensitivity, Intercultural Communicative Competence, along with many others.

16 "Interpathy is intentional cognitive and affective envisioning of the thoughts and imagining the feelings of a truly separate Other as they occur in another world of reality—another culture, another worldview, another epistemology." David Augsburger, writing in 2014, tells of the origins of the word in 1986, by his Indonesian colleague Dr. Willie Toisuta. David Augsburger, 'Interpathy Re-Envisioned: Reflecting on Observed Practice of Mutuality by Counselors Who Muddle along Cultural Boundaries or Are Thrown into a Wholly Strange Location', *Reflective Practice: Formation and Supervision in Ministry* 34 (2014): 11–22.

17 Karl Rahner, *The Love of Jesus and the Love of Neighbor* (Crossroad Publishing Company, 1983), 71–83.

18 James 1:26 NLT

19 1 John 2:9 NLT

20 Micah 6:8 NIV

21 Cultural Intelligence Center, ed., 'Domestic CQ' (Cultural Intelligence Center, 5 July 2021), https://culturalq.com/about-cultural-intelligence/domestic-cq/.

22 CQ Model is property of the Cultural Intelligence Center. David A. Livermore, *Cultural Intelligence: Improving Your CQ to Engage Our Multicultural World*, Youth, Family, and Culture Series (Grand Rapids, Mich.: Baker Academic, 2009). See also https://culturalq.com/about-cultural-intelligence/culture/. Livermore's original CQ diagram had 'love' as the centre, with the description that CQ is moving from desiring to love the other, to having the ability to do so.

23 There are many courses, books and workshops that are designed to help you grow in CQ. Like EQ, often what is most helpful is having a skilled person guide you.

24 The term was first used by Dr. Melanie Tervalon and Dr. Jann Murray-Garcia in 1998.

25 Melanie Tervalon, and Jann Murray-García, "Cultural Humility Versus Cultural Competence: A Critical Distinction in Defining Physician Training Outcomes in Multicultural Education," *Journal Of Health Care for the Poor and Underserved* 9, no. 2 (1998): 1.

26 J. S, 'Intercultural Living - Cultural Humility' (Self-Study workbook, Singapore, 2017).

27 Louise Giesbrecht, 'Defining Intercultural Competence', Web video, 2013, https://www.youtube.com/watch?v=SJqBhLgSNQY.

Step 3: Embracing Appropriate Self-care

1 Hay et al., 150. Mitchell, 266. Burns et al devote two whole chapters to self-care of pastors. Burns, Chapman, and Guthrie, 60-100. Lee and Fredrickson focus on care for our physical bodies. Lee, and Fredrickson, 108-27.

2 Meryem Brown, 'Navigating Mental Health as a Christian', podcast, Word of Life, accessed 18 May 2021, https://wayoflifepodcast.podbean.com/e/episode-6-1621300596/.

3 Viktor E. Frankl, *Man's Search For Meaning: The Classic Tribute to Hope from the Holocaust* (Ebury Publishing, 2013), 75, https://books.google.com.au/books?id=EbltAAAAQBAJ.

4 Edith Eger, *The Choice: A True Story of Hope* (Ebury Publishing, 2017), https://books.google.com.au/books?id=uBwZDAAAQBAJ.

5 Kanowski, 'Ben Crowe'.

6 Don Allsman, 'Day 3: Jesus Had a Different Objective', *Loving Jesus More: 40 Days Devotional Series* (blog), 15 August 2021, https://www.bible.com/en-GB/reading-plans/27331-loving-jesus-more/day/3.

7 Eurich's article has helpful insights if you would like to explore these more. http://thebusinessleadership.academy/wp-content/uploads/2019/08/What-Self-Awareness-Really-Is-and-How-to-Cultivate-It.pdf

8 Tasha Eurich, 'What Self-Awareness Really Is (and How to Cultivate

It)', *Harvard Business Review*, 2018, http://thebusinessleadership.academy/wp-content/uploads/2019/08/What-Self-Awareness-Really-Is-and-How-to-Cultivate-It.pdf.

9   Kanowski, 'Ben Crowe'.

10 William David Taylor, Antonia Van der Meer, and Reg Reimer, *Sorrow and Blood: Christian Mission in Contexts of Suffering, Persecution, and Martyrdom* (Pasadena: William Carey Library, 2012), xxii. Rae Jean Proeschold-Bell and Jason Byassee, *Faithful and Fractured: Responding to the Clergy Health Crisis* (Grand Rapids: Baker Academic, 2018), 93, 116.

11 Patricia Miersma, 'Counseling Victims of Human-Induced Trauma', in *Sorrow and Blood : Christian Mission in Contexts of Suffering, Persecution, and Martyrdom*, ed. William David Taylor (Pasadena: William Carey Library, 2012), 455. Rob Hay et al., *Worth Keeping : Global Perspectives on Best Practice in Missionary Retention*, Globalization of Mission Series (Pasadena, Calif.: William Carey Library, 2007), 221, 319.

12 This extremely useful concept I gleaned from David & Susan Nikles in 2017. Dr. D Nikles and S Nikles, *Cycles of Transformation*, 2nd edition (Australia: Christian Wholeness Framework, 2010). Nikles adapted Warlow's original model. For application in a ministry context see Proeschold-Bell and Byassee, *Faithful and Fractured: Responding to the Clergy Health Crisis*, 128, 29, 53. Lee and Fredrickson call this "nurturing healthy relationships." Cameron Lee and Kurt Fredrickson, *That Their Work Will Be a Joy : Understanding and Coping with the Challenges of Pastoral Ministry* (Wipf and Stock Publishers, 2012), 148–69. For application in an Australian Baptist context, see Keith Mitchell, 'Sustainability in Ministry and the Prevention of Dropout for Australian Baptist Pastors Serving in Local Church- Based Ministries' (Sydney, University of Technology Sydney, 2020), 273–74.

13 Lee and Fredrickson, *That Their Work Will Be a Joy*, 128–47. Proeschold-Bell and Byassee, *Faithful and Fractured: Responding to the Clergy Health Crisis*, 131, 34, 39, 62. Peter Brain, *Going the Distance*, Second edition, How to Stay Fit for a Lifetime of Ministry (Australia: Matthias Media, 2020), loc 586, 87.

14 B. Brown, *The Gifts of Imperfection: Let Go of Who You Think You're Supposed to Be and Embrace Who You Are* (Hazelden Publishing, 2010).

15 Brain, *Going the Distance*, loc 283, 511, 39, 88.

16 There are many resources available regarding signs of burnout, and appropriate responses. Some of the signs of burnout include: feeling exhausted and unable to perform basic tasks; losing motivation in many aspects of your life, including your work and friendships; feeling unable to focus or concentrate on tasks; feeling empty or lacking in emotion; losing your passion and drive; experiencing conflict in your relationships with co-workers, friends and family; withdrawing emotionally from friends and family. Reach Out Australia, 'What Is Burnout?' (Reach Out Australia, 2021), https://au.reachout.com/articles/burnout-and-chronic-stress. For a more detailed list, see Ulrich Kraft, 'Burned Out', *Scientific American Mind* 17, no. 3 (2006): 31. See also https://www.mindtools.com/pages/article/avoiding-burnout.htm?utm_source=cons_nl&utm_medium=email&utm_campaign=dd-rampup-email2&utm_content=burnout_cta1&dm_i=6R80,6AIX,2GOPQV,Q812,1

17 Brain, *Going the Distance*, loc 423. Mitchell describes the experience of Australian Baptist pastors who have continued in ministry through a time of a near-burnout, highlighting the significance of a supportive external source and resulting growth in self-awareness. Mitchell, 'Sustainability in Ministry', 265.

18 These are from the Living Bible, TLB.

Conclusion

1 Stephen Hoke, William David Taylor, and Stephen Hoke, *Global Mission Handbook : A Guide for Crosscultural Service* (Downers Grove, Ill.: IVP Books, 2009), 289.

2 Anglican Church of Australia General Synod, *A Prayer Book for Australia: For Use Together with the Book of Common Prayer (1662) and an Australian Prayer Book (1978)*, ed. E. J. Dwyer (Mulgrave: Broughton Books, 1996).

Appendix

1 Kelly S O'Donnell, ed., *Doing Member Care Well: Perspectives and Practices From Around the World*, Globalization of Mission Series (Pasadena, Calif.: William Carey Library, 2002), 3.

2 Brain, *Going the Distance*, loc 115.

3 Miersma, 'Counseling Victims', 9.
4 Brain, *Going the Distance*, loc 163.
5 "The gravity of the work of a pastor is reflected in the ordination charges of different churches." Brain, loc 95. See also Proeschold-Bell and Byassee, *Faithful and Fractured: Responding to the Clergy Health Crisis*, 25.
6 Balswick, King, and Reimer, *The Reciprocating Self; Scazzero, Emotionally Healthy Spirituality*.
7 Brain, *Going the Distance*, loc 29, 198-99, 204, 09-10.
8 Proeschold-Bell and Byassee, *Faithful and Fractured: Responding to the Clergy Health Crisis*, loc 199, p 3.
9 This includes simply overeating and under-exercise, leading to many physical health complications, as clearly outlined in Faithful and Fractured and also Resilient Ministry. Proeschold-Bell and Byassee, *Faithful and Fractured: Responding to the Clergy Health Crisis*; Burns, Chapman, and Guthrie, *Resilient Ministry: What Pastors Told Us About Surviving And Thriving*.
10 This is seen in many writings, including Hay et al., Worth Keeping; Kraft, 'Burned Out'; Mitchell, 'Sustainability in Ministry'; Proeschold-Bell and Byassee, *Faithful and Fractured: Responding to the Clergy Health Crisis*.
11 Kraft, 'Burned Out', 31.
12 Proeschold-Bell and Byassee, *Faithful and Fractured: Responding to the Clergy Health Crisis*, 18, 23.
13 Balswick, King, and Reimer, *The Reciprocating Self*, 99.
14 This is shown in the survey results from the University of Western Sydney. Grant Bickerton et al., 'Well-Being in Ministry Results Overview' (Sydney: University of Western Sydney, N.D.). See https://summitlife.org/an-audience-of-one-summitlife-today-september-14-2015/

www.ingramcontent.com/pod-product-compliance
Lightning Source LLC
Chambersburg PA
CBHW020327010526
44107CB00054B/2014